# Little Kids, Big Dilemm Main June 2018

Psychologist Dr Sarah Kuppen, expert in early child development, uses her scientific expertise to sort through the hype and give you the facts. Using the latest developmental research, she provides practical tips and solves more than 50 familiar parent questions and dilemmas. Inside you will find advice on:

- five ways to tame a tantrum
- what to do if your child isn't talking
- the scientific facts on breastfeeding versus formula feeding
- managing sibling fights and conflict.

*Little Kids, Big Dilemmas* is an essential guide for science-minded parents and childcare professionals alike. Reading this book will allow you to make informed decisions on the big topics for parenting in the early years.

**Sarah Kuppen, PhD CPsychol,** is a Senior Lecturer in Developmental Psychology at Anglia Ruskin University and a mother of two little boys. Originally a teacher, she gained her PhD from the Centre for Neuroscience in Education at Cambridge University and now specialises in early child development. In addition to her academic work, she regularly gives public talks, appears in the media, works as a consultant, and runs parenting workshops at Cambridge University's Institute of Continuing Education.

# Little Kids, Big Dilemmas

Your Parenting Problems
Solved by Science

## Sarah Kuppen

 Routledge
Taylor & Francis Group

LONDON AND NEW YORK

First published 2018
by Routledge
2 Park Square, Milton Park, Abingdon, Oxon OX14 4RN

and by Routledge
711 Third Avenue, New York, NY 10017

*Routledge is an imprint of the Taylor & Francis Group, an informa business*

© 2018 Sarah Kuppen

*British Library Cataloguing in Publication Data*
A catalogue record for this book is available from the British Library

*Library of Congress Cataloging in Publication Data*
A catalog record has been requested for this book

ISBN: 978-1-138-85790-2 (hbk)
ISBN: 978-1-138-85791-9 (pbk)
ISBN: 978-1-315-71835-4 (ebk)

Typeset in Times New Roman
by Keystroke, Neville Lodge, Tettenhall, Wolverhampton

This book is dedicated to my family: Stefan, Alex, Ollie, Peter and Rebecca

# Contents

# Introduction

I have always been a seeker of facts, and never more so than at the arrival of my first child. Pass-the-day kind of chat on nappies, weaning or strollers wasn't for me. I wanted the research based evidence on the major parenting issues. If I struggled to breastfeed, would it impact long term on the health and well-being of my child? If I let my child cry herself to sleep, was I a bad mum? As a developmental psychologist, with a good grounding in the science of child development, I wanted more than just opinion.

The parenting section of my local bookshop was no help. These books were all about the guru. While I could see that much of the writing reflected received opinion, their advice came from personal experience, and the anecdotes of those around them. They used a sample size of one, or maybe three at the most. I wanted evidence based advice. And by that, I mean I wanted advice based on published research evidence, from peer reviewed journals.

Clearly, that book hadn't yet been written. So I set out to do the research myself. I gathered my parenting questions, the questions of my friends, colleagues, online groups and pretty much anyone with young children who would talk to me. I put them together and then painstakingly looked up the relevant papers. I made summaries and lists of everything, and it took up nearly all of my spare time for about four years.

While researching the book was a hugely enriching experience, it also reminded me of some things. For one, the evidence out there is largely based on English speaking mothers. Also, some of it is poor quality. That's because, with parenting, it's hard to establish cause and effect. So, in return, lots of assumptions and short cuts are made.

It's easier to explain what I mean using an example. One that comes up a lot is spanking. Spanking your child is a questionable practice, and not one that I'd advocate. However, I don't know if it makes your child more aggressive. The reason I don't know is because the studies have been inconclusive. Even for the purposes of research, we can't take a random group of parents and tell them to spank their children. It's not ethical. However, when we recruit spanking and non-spanking parents from the population, and compare their kids, it's not a good test.

For one, the groups have important differences. Parents who spank are likely to have higher aggression than those who don't. Due to shared genes, their children may also be more aggressive. While some sloppy research could draw a line between the higher levels of child aggression and spanking, the study has been poorly controlled. Because the shared genes between parent and child have not been considered, we're no closer to a conclusion. Furthermore, how do we know that the relationship only goes one way? More aggressive children are likely to demonstrate more anti-social behaviours, and may therefore be more likely to receive disciplining consequences such as spanking. But, many media outlets don't apply a critical approach. Attention grabbing headlines always win out – Research Says Spanking Makes Your Child More Aggressive! Parents may then see this as definitive.

One goal of this book is to provide a hype-free guide for parents, carers or people working with young children. There is a large amount of rigorous research out there, which can be illuminating and helpful. Knowing whether sleep training programmes work (they do), whether to use them (it's a personal choice), how to get your child off to a flying start (talk to her), and how to tame your child's tantrums (be prepared) are incredibly helpful and reassuring.

You don't need me to tell you that caring for a young child is both thrilling and exasperating. Writing this book gave me a knowledge base that genuinely made things easier. I took comfort in large studies and appreciated the context they provided. I also valued the view I gained behind the headlines. Now, having written it all down, I hope it is of use to you. We are all told how quickly a child's first years pass by. I hope this book will minimise the stress. I hope it will provide you with options and alternatives. Ultimately, I hope it will allow you more time and freedom to enjoy those great moments. The ones that make spending time with a young child such a life enhancing experience.

Note: You'll already have noticed, I use *she* throughout, and I also often refer to the reader as a parent, even though I mean parent/carer/guardian or adult who works with young children. Both shortcuts are for readability and I hope you will excuse them.

Becky Cameron

# 1 Help! Toddler tantrums are making my life miserable!

---

**Parent post – toddler tantrums**

*My two and a half year old is testing me to the limit. He throws mighty tantrums! I can't control him. Often he will hit me in the face, throw himself around on the ground, kick and scream. Last week he managed to escape from our playgroup, because someone left the door open. When I eventually found him and tried to bring him back, I couldn't stop him screaming. Yesterday, after I had told him off for something, he ran out of the front door and hid in the garden. I felt so worried; I ended up being consoled by a complete stranger on our street. His behaviour is making me crazy and I know feeling this way isn't making things any better. I need help!*

---

Tantrums! We all hate them. Particularly the ones where everyone's watching! Standing by while your two year old puts on a show for everyone isn't much fun. You feel helpless and incompetent and just want it to end. But what can you do?

Understanding what's going on can help. Knowing it's not just you, that all parents face these difficult moments, makes it feel less personal. Tantrums are little (or big) explosions of uncontrolled emotion. While we don't enjoy them, they are perfectly normal for young children. Most children under four are not equipped to deal with the strong feelings brought on by daily life. For most children, tantrums are an inevitable part of growing up. Knowing how to minimise and deal with them once they've got started is essential.

## Five ways to tame a tantrum

1   **Enhance your calm and be prepared.**

A tantrum isn't just about your child's behaviour, it's about your state of mind too. As in the parent post earlier, if you're stressed, pressed for time, feeling awkward or embarrassed, you likely won't be feeling sensitive, warm, empathic, considerate, patient etc. etc. Or in other words, you won't be at your best and you won't be behaving in the way that gets the best out of your child. The message here is to **be organised, plan ahead and leave time** for contingencies. Being prepared means you will deal better with the tricky situations that arise. Prevention is the most reliable method to deal with a tantrum – use all appropriate means at your disposal and don't let it get started.

2   **Avoid unnecessary confrontation.**

If your child is tired, hungry or ill, leave it. This is not the time for a battle of wills. If you can, just move things along and get things done without a big confrontation; **leave the disciplining discussions until the time is right**.

3   **Use distraction.**

Distraction is a parent's best friend. When things start getting tense and you recognise the onset of a meltdown, pick something, anything, that you think might interest your child and **redirect her attention**. Depending on where you are and what you're doing, get your phone out and call someone – maybe granny or a sibling, suggest a snack, story or some time outside. Music can be a handy tool to change the mood.

4   **Provide an explanation.**

If you are parenting a preschooler, **explain yourself**. Four year olds will appreciate an explanation as to why you're asking for whatever it is. Even if the reasoning is well known, a reminder and a chance for your child to listen to you talking it through again can help. 'Sam you know we don't bang our cutlery on the table. Doing this can damage the table as well as the knife. Also, your brother and sisters and I don't like the noise and it spoils the nice feeling we have when we're eating together.'

5   **If a tantrum has started, let it run its course.**

If your child's tantrum is in full throw, just leave her to it. **Don't try to appease, make deals, bribes and threats or talk her through it.** Just make sure that she is somewhere safe where she can't hurt herself or anyone else and isn't going to damage any property. Keep an eye on her, but do feel free to leave the room if it will help your sanity. When researchers looked at the components of tantrums and how long they lasted, they found something of great interest. When parents intervened when a child was in full tantrum, it took longer for the tantrum to finish (Potegal, Kosorok, & Davidson, 2003). So, it doesn't matter what you say or do, if your child is safe and you want the tantrum over, don't engage. Wait it out.

## The science of tantrums in young children

### *Why do toddlers have tantrums?*

It won't surprise you to hear that tantrums are an expression of anger and FRUSTRATION! Your child may also feed sadness, often linked to disappointment about not getting her own way.

Screaming, kicking, hitting and stiffening are considered to be high intensity emotion. Yelling and throwing are deemed to be more moderate, while stomping is a mild expression of frustration in most children. Snivelling, whining and crying can also appear towards the end of a tantrum, and are most usually an expression of sadness.

So why do almost all children go through a period of having frequent tantrums? And why does this occur around the ages of two and three? The answers can be found in how a child's brain develops.

As we get older, we learn to modify our primary feelings of anger through processes of rationalisation, reappraisal and suppression or inhibition. In other words, we learn how to not get too bothered about things. Or at least we learn how to not show how bothered we are.

Keeping our emotions in check, or socially appropriate, involves high order thinking processes. These networks develop much later than those for primary emotions, such as anger or fear. Because of this mismatch, many children lack the skills to manage their intense feelings. This is particularly evident over the ages of two and three, where children experience a strong desire for independence and control. The frustrations brought on by the continual testing of boundaries can mean frequent emotional meltdowns.

## Disciplining

### *Good discipline*

'So how do you discipline your two year old?' says one friend to another. What she really means is: 'What kind of punishments do you use and do they work?' While many of us take discipline to mean punishment, psychologists understand disciplining as a much larger set of behaviours.

For, along with negative consequences, parents do a great deal of explaining and patient modelling of good, friendly, pro-social behaviours. Whether intentional or not, parents guide their children through a process of social and moral education. This is at the heart of disciplining.

In the early years, we support our impulse driven toddlers with the aim of developing school ready four year olds. We hope to have a skilled, (at least partly) self-controlled preschooler who is eager to learn and to make friends. However, disciplining does not end in childhood. It defines our role as parents.

There is no recipe for good discipline. Your child is an individual and what goes down well with one may flop with another. Keeping this in mind, research has highlighted some features that characterise parent/child relationships where the foundations of mutual respect and pro-social behaviour are well established.

*Be emotionally warm*

We all know people who are emotionally warm. They smile, maybe touch you lightly on the shoulder or arm when you are talking. They tune in, really listen to you and maybe even validate your feelings by nodding, or mirroring, for example responding with similar phrases or thoughts and feelings. As adults, we like to be acknowledged, listened to and respected. As children, we feel the same. Showing emotional warmth allows children to relax in the knowledge that their needs will be met. Showing empathy, compassion, respect and emotional warmth means your child is in a good place to return those feelings and respect your wishes. This will be particularly helpful when things get tense and stressful. When it is all you can do to muster a please and you just want it done, it may be helpful to try showing love or warmth in your requests. Emotional warmth and love is *the* defining feature of our relationship with our children (Howard, 1996). Using kind humour can also work wonders!

*Model good behaviour*

Do as I say and not as I do won't cut it with kids. Children learn best from the people that they like and care about, so we need to set a good example. Social learning theory (Bandura, 1977) suggests that if our children see us keeping a lid on our frustrations, doing a good bit of cleaning up, having healthy social habits, or whatever it is, they are more likely to follow suit.

*Be consistent*

Being soft on poor behaviour one day and hard the next is confusing for children. Boundaries need to be clear, as do consequences. But sometimes it's not that easy. In periods of stress, depression or isolation, it can be hard to be consistent. We may not feel physically or emotionally up for confrontation. We might let things go where we shouldn't, or be too harsh. A supportive network of friends, family or a partner can work wonders in helping us to get the right balance again and again. Consistently treating our children with warmth, sensitivity and care is a good indication that we are in control of our own emotions and emotionally available to our children.

*Show empathy*

Empathy is the ability to recognise and share the feelings of others. It is a key component of strong parent/child relationships. Many parents share in the emotions experienced by their child. If we listen and respond to our children appropriately and show our understanding of their feelings, emotional closeness is likely to grow.

Adopting an empathic viewpoint means seeing life from our child's point of view. This may help with disciplining. Taking a child's perspective can help to identify necessary boundaries without imposing excessive or unnecessary restrictions. Always saying no can degrade the quality of a parent and child relationship. In the early years, creating a strong bond between parent and child means that there should be a great deal of shared excitement, discovery and exploration. Where possible, focus on encouraging and praising. Parental empathy and related characteristics such as sympathy, understanding, acceptance, as well as general sensitivity, are thought to be strongly beneficial to a child's social and emotional development (Eisenberg & Miller, 1987).

*Be attentive*

Family playtime can be a great moment for lavishing attention on young children. A joint activity, or just being next to each other, means it's easy to pay close attention to your child and you can give immediate feedback. Providing undivided attention can produce feelings of togetherness and may support your child's self-esteem as she feels valued and important. In families facing difficulties, time set aside for individual positive attention has helped to lower the frequency of tantrums (Thelen, 1979).

*Talk it through*

If you have a toddler, a straightforward request may be the most effective route to getting out the door. However, preschoolers will often appreciate an explanation, which may also make them more likely to comply. Children of this age also like to have the consequences of unwanted behaviour explained to them, or even demonstrated. For example, one study asked mums to model the consequences of unwanted behaviour to their children. In this case, the consequence was the child being ignored for a short period of time. Children who received the ignoring demonstration were more likely to comply with requests (Davies et al., 1984). Of course, whether or not this lasted beyond the experiment we don't know!

*Use your stern face for toddlers*

While it might be tempting at times, shouting at toddlers is most often counter-productive. The shout can often energise children into action, whether it is the desired action or not (Blum et al., 1995). Telling your toddler the same thing over and over again, without any change in consequences, is also not helpful. Essentially you are telling your toddler that if she doesn't do this thing, nothing will happen. Your request loses meaning if repeated too many times. A more effective technique is to state your wish once and then silently look at your child with a stern face. If she associates the stern face with consequences that she doesn't like, then you are more likely to be successful.

*Positive reinforcement*

Giving positive feedback is a very effective way to encourage wanted behaviours in your child. Positive feedback can be a touch, hug, smile, wink, high five, anything that the child will take as approval. If you prefer, positive reinforcement can also be achieved through using star charts or rewards such as stories, games or other forms of time together. The goal of positive reinforcement is for your child to feel pride or happiness in having behaved well. One way this can be done is to give your child a positive label that they can identify with. For example, research has shown that children who were offered the chance to be a good 'helper', rather than just help out, were more likely to behave pro-socially (Bryan, Master, & Walton, 2014). Positive reinforcement is by far the most common disciplining technique used by parents. It makes both parents and children feel good.

## Parent post – red flag tantrums

*My four year old is having frequent tantrums, about two to three per day, much more than she used to have when she was in the 'terrible twos'. The other day she had a tantrum because she refused to brush her teeth. When she has a tantrum she can bang her head on the wall, scratch herself and will scream and cry for up to 15 minutes. She finds it very difficult to calm herself down and we usually have to put the television on to bring her out of it. We never give into her tantrums so we don't know why she keeps throwing them. We're worried that she may have some sort of developmental issue. How do we know when we should go seek some help?*

## Can tantrums be a sign of developmental problems?

Tantrums in young children are part of normal development and reflect a maturing brain. However, there are some red flags to watch out for. You may wish to see a health specialist if tantrums persist beyond the preschool years, or if your child's tantrums are particularly disruptive to your everyday life. Self-injurious behaviour, such as if your child bites or scratches herself, may be of particular concern and should be followed up with a clinical practitioner.

## Frequently asked questions – disciplining

### How can I get my child to behave well?

For most children, praising the good and ignoring the bad will not be an adequate strategy for achieving socially desirable behaviour. One study showed that when wanted behaviours were praised, and unwanted behaviours ignored, children became more, rather than less, anti-social over time (Herbert et al., 1973). For most kids, a consistent consequence routine provides the most reliable route to achieving pro-social behaviour.

Studies focusing on two and three year olds, specifically, have found a combination of explanation and time outs works best to reduced unwanted behaviours (Larzelere et al., 1996). Using both together is more effective than the use of spanking, hand slapping or withdrawing privileges for children of this age. Using a warning system, where the child is given at least one chance to change her behaviour, reduces the number of time outs needed. This is important, as disciplining consequences become less impactful, the more often they are used.

While time out is the most widely used and researched technique, many other disciplining options are available to parents. For example, depending on the situation, showing disapproval through a 'don't do that', or unhappy face, might be enough to stop the unwanted behaviour. Alternatively, the removal of favoured activities or the addition of unpopular tasks may be a good choice for behaviours that are really causing you or the family difficulties. Below are some techniques you could try if you aren't already.

Some common consequences for unwanted behaviour:

- verbal disapproval – however, remember that this gives the child attention for being naughty;
- privilege withdrawal – this can be anything from forfeiting computer/television time to taking away a favoured toy;
- logical consequences – same as above but the punishment is related to the unwanted behaviour. So, for example, if two children are fighting over taking turns with a game, the game could be taken away for a period of time.
- nonverbal disapproval – looking stern or glaring. This is most effective if it's clear that the child is looking at you and there is a history of stern looks being followed by consequences as outlined above.

### How do you do time outs?

Time outs can either be seen as a negative consequence (being removed from the pleasant company of others, or an enjoyed activity) or as quiet time for reflection after some unwanted behaviour has occurred. In children under school age, although you may wish time out to be the latter, realistically it may be difficult for your child to calm herself down. Thinking things through may not always be a realistic expectation in these situations.

## Under twos (but not younger than one)

When administering a time out, it's best to catch the unwanted behaviour as it's happening and say something like: 'Sophie, please don't pull the cat's tail, it hurts her and isn't kind.' If she doesn't stop, then give a warning: 'Right, stop that right now.' If she still hasn't stopped: 'I'm going to count to three and if you keep grabbing her tail, I'm going to put you to sit in the corner.' (Replace with any location that is appropriate, but at this age it shouldn't be somewhere too far away.)

Put her into the corner with something appropriate to look at or play with. If she has calmed down when moved, give her some praise, but, even if not, try to redirect her attention on to another activity. Children this age are usually easily distracted and can often be quickly comforted, with the incident forgotten.

Time outs at this age are more about giving your child a change of scene or removing her from the situation. Attempting to get her to sit quietly or in one place isn't likely to be successful and you will end up chasing her around the house. Although she might enjoy this game, more traditional time outs are left until she is slightly older.

## Time outs in two to fours

Time outs in this age range are about providing some cooling down time. As discussed earlier, they can also be viewed as a negative consequence, with your child removed from your reinforcing attention and company. Putting your child in a separate room provides a powerful message about the need for acceptable behaviour when she is with you, or others, in the house.

In order for time out to be effective, there needs to be a good level of time in. This is time where the child is given lots of positive attention and reinforcement. The difference between time in and time out will be very noticeable to her, and she will want to return to the social atmosphere and your company.

Time out needs to take place in a quiet and uninteresting location. Often a cot or bedroom can be best. Although at first your child may just leave from wherever you put her, after she realises that you'll only put her back again, she will likely stay put. A timer can help with this, for example something where she can see the time elapsing (like a traditional sand egg timer). The common advice is that time outs should last as long as your child's age, so that would be under five minutes for this age group. A short break is best, particularly if your child is upset. It is kind to offer a cuddle or some show of physical affection after the time out has taken place.

### Should I spank my child?

Until recently, spanking was a popular way for parents to respond to unwanted behaviour from children. These days, it is more common for parents to prefer other methods, such as time out or privilege withdrawal (Ipsos Mori, 2007). In many countries the corporal punishment of children has been deemed unethical and has been banned.

The decline in parental spanking may be linked to a more general move away from physical aggression, a belief that other methods are more effective or a concern over inflicting psychological harm. While some studies have drawn links between spanking and aggressive behaviour in children (MacKenzie et al., 2013), a causal link is very difficult to prove. A parent who is more aggressive may spank her child and she may also have children who are more aggressive. Whether the aggression in the child is due to shared genes or parenting behaviours, or even more likely an interaction between the two factors, is very difficult to tease apart. The influence of genes needs to be controlled before any claims about the effect of spanking on children can be made.

## Resources

All website URLs in the book were accessed in November 2017.

Bandura, A. (1977). *Social Learning Theory*. Englewood Cliffs, NJ: Prentice Hall.

Blum, N. J., Williams, G. E., Friman, P. C., & Christophersen, E. R. (1995). Disciplining young children: The role of verbal instructions and reasoning. *Pediatrics*, *96*(2), 336–341.

Bryan, C. J., Master, A., & Walton, G. M. (2014). 'Helping' versus 'being a helper': Invoking the self to increase helping in young children. *Child Development*, *85*(5), 1836–1842. http://doi.org/10.1111/cdev.12244

Davies, G. R., McMahon, R. J., Flessati, E. W., & Tiedemann, G. L. (1984). Verbal rationales and modeling as adjuncts to a parenting technique for child compliance. *Child Development*, *55*(4), 1290. http://doi.org/10.2307/1129998

Eisenberg, N., & Miller, P. A. (1987). The relation of empathy to prosocial and related behaviors. *Psychological Bulletin, 101*(1), 91–119.

Herbert, E. W., Pinkston, E. M., Hayden, M. L., Sajwaj, T. E., Pinkston, S., Cordua, G., & Jackson, C. (1973). Adverse effects of differential parental attention. *Journal of Applied Behavior Analysis, 6*(1), 15–30. http://doi.org/10.1901/jaba.1973.6-15

Howard, B. (1996). Advising parents on discipline: What works. *Pediatrics, 98*(4), 809.

Ipsos Mori. (2007). A study into the views of parents on the physical punishment of children for the Department for Children, Schools and Families (DCSF). http://dera.ioe.ac.uk/6886/8/Section%2058%20Parental%20Survey.pdf

Larzelere, R. E., Schneider, W. N., Larson, D. B., & Pike, P. L. (1996). The effects of discipline responses in delaying toddler misbehavior recurrences. *Child & Family Behavior Therapy, 18*(3), 35–57.

MacKenzie, M. J., Nicklas, E., Waldfogel, J., & Brooks-Gunn, J. (2013). Spanking and child development across the first decade of life. *Pediatrics, 132*(5), e1118-1125. http://doi.org/10.1542/peds.2013-1227

Potegal, M., Kosorok, M. R., & Davidson, R. J. (2003). Temper tantrums in young children: 2. Tantrum duration and temporal organization. *Journal of Developmental & Behavioral Pediatrics, 24*(3), 148–154. http://doi.org/10.1097/00004703-200306000-00003

Thelen, M. H. (1979). Treatment of temper tantrum behavior by means of noncontingent positive attention. *Journal of Clinical Child Psychology, 8*(2), 140.

Becky Cameron

# 2   How can I get more sleep?

---

**Parent post – lack of sleep**

*I can no longer cope with my current levels of sleep deprivation. It's certainly affecting my productivity, but also my mental and emotional health. I remember going through two and a half years of bad sleep with my eldest and just suffering through. Now, with more work responsibility and further demands on my time, I can't face going through this again. How can I get more sleep? My baby is ten months old.*

---

New baby in the house? As any new parent will tell you, you're going to be tired. Broken nights and new routines mean that sleep isn't what it used to be. But at what point might we reasonably expect a full night's sleep and can we make this day come any sooner? Is sleep training the answer?

## What is sleep training, should I use it, and will it work?

Sleep training is a topic which divides opinion. Only you will know the best solution for getting the sleep you require, while respecting the needs of your baby and others at home. Some children will fall into good, easy patterns of sleep on their own. However, many others will struggle, either with falling asleep or getting back to sleep after waking. Your response provides the key to establishing a good night's sleep for you and your child. Sleep training programmes establish new expectations and routines around sleep.

A number of sleep training programmes have been developed to help parents regulate child sleep. As these programmes vary greatly in their approach, there is one to suit most parents, even those who feel uncomfortable letting their child cry at night. Three strategies are listed below. The first is provided for information purposes only, as it is not recommended as an appropriate approach. However, all three programmes have demonstrated effectiveness in minimising difficulties at bedtime in healthy children. They also promote self-soothing behaviours and reduce long night time awakenings (Guilleminault et al., 2003).

### Cry it out

In the cry it out method, children are left to cry until they fall asleep. As parents are advised to ignore their child completely, it is not recommended as best practice by health professionals. A child left to cry *will* eventually fall asleep through exhaustion. If left to cry every night, she will eventually cry less and less, as she learns that crying does not bring anyone. While effective, many parents feel uncomfortable allowing their child to cry for long periods of time. It may also be unsafe, as your child may be crying because she is unwell or in distress, and should not be left without checking.

### Controlled crying (progressive waiting or graduated extinction)

This technique falls under a number of different names. However, they all share the common requirement that parents need to wait for increasingly long intervals before checking on their child. The best known proponent of the technique is Richard Ferber (Ferber, 1985). A typical example of progressive waiting would look something like this:

After putting to bed (or when waking in the night), if your child begins to cry:

Day 1 – wait 3 minutes and then go in; second cry, wait 5 minutes; third cry, 7 minutes; subsequent cries, 10 minutes
Day 2 – first 5 mins; second 7 mins; third 10 mins; subsequent 12 mins
Day 3 – first 10 mins; second 12 mins; third 15 mins; subsequent 15 mins

In the controlled crying technique, going in to check and comfort does not last longer than two minutes. In these checking periods, children are given only minimal attention. Something like replacing a blanket that has slipped off is allowed. However, picking up an object that has been thrown is not. From Day 4 onwards, waiting episodes increase by a couple of minutes each day, until reaching a maximum wait of 30 minutes. By Day 7 it is suggested that the progressive waiting programme will usually have been successful. By this point Dr Ferber suggests that your child will have developed some strategies for getting herself to sleep and will no longer regularly be waking in the night needing your attention. Where the programme is not effective, help should be sought from a medical practitioner.

### Camping out

In camping out, the parent gradually removes herself from the child's bedroom and then periodically checks in. To begin with, a chair should be placed next to your baby's cot. The baby can then be stroked or rocked to sleep. When she is sleeping, you can then leave the room. After a few nights of falling to sleep like this, the routine is changed slightly, so that you no longer stroke or rock the child to sleep. Again, after a few nights, the routine is changed. In the next variation, the parent sits slightly away from the bed. Over time, the parent gradually moves away from the bed until she no longer needs to be in the room. If the baby wakes up during the night, the chair can be returned to the most recent location. The baby should be comforted with minimum stroking or rocking and should only be lifted up if very distressed. Over time (on average three weeks), your child should be able to be left on her own and settle herself to sleep.

## Will sleep training hurt my child?

Some parents may feel intuitively that it is wrong to leave their child to cry, even for a short period of time. In this case, the camping out technique (described above) may work best. However, claims that allowing children to cry for short periods of time will cause emotional damage, or have long term mental health implications, are not supported by research. Well controlled research suggests that using a sleep programme that is sensitive to the needs and age of the child is not related to any particular developmental outcomes. One study, which presents this conclusion, examined a large number of families involved in an Australian sleep project. As part of this project, parents administered sleep training programmes such as progressive waiting and camping out. The children receiving these programmes were followed up five years later. No differences were found between the project and comparison children on measures of emotional and conduct behaviour, sleep habits, social functioning, stress or child–parent closeness and attachment (Price et al., 2012). In fact, clinical studies have demonstrated a positive relationship between the use of sleep interventions for children with sleep difficulties and maternal mental health. Mothers of children with severe sleep difficulties have experienced reduced depression after the introduction of a sleep training programme (Hiscock & Wake, 2002).

## How do sleep training programmes work?

Sleep training programmes work by encouraging the child to fall asleep without assistance. Gradually, the parent makes herself unavailable for longer periods of time, requiring the child to develop her own self-soothing and settling behaviours.

The psychological principle used is graduated extinction, which comes from the theory of classical conditioning (Pavlov, 1927). In conditioning, an association is made between two things, one of which is biologically important. So, for example, in Pavlov's very famous experiment with the salivating dogs, a pairing is made between the sound of the bell and the appearance of food. While some parents may not feel comfortable with this process, in graduated extinction, the child begins to realise that if she cries, an adult won't immediately appear. The association between crying at night and an adult appearing has been broken. This means that when she is feeling upset at night, your child is less likely to cry immediately and more likely to try self-comforting strategies first.

---

### Parent post – SIDS

*I know it doesn't make sense, but I get really anxious that my eight month old is going to stop breathing. I go in to check her at night. If I can't immediately see that she's breathing, my heart starts to pound. Sometimes I go in and she has rolled over onto her tummy. I put her on her back, but then worry that she may roll over again in the night. Is there something I can do to make her stay on her back? I know it is the recommended position to reduce the risk of SIDS and I get really worried.*

---

## Sudden infant death syndrome (SIDS)

Sudden infant death syndrome (SIDS), sometimes known as cot death, is the sudden and unexplained death of an apparently healthy child. SIDS is more common in boys and most often occurs within the first three months of life. While there are no known underlying causes of SIDS, there are a number of factors that are related to increased risk. If the child was born with low weight or prematurely, if she is placed to sleep on her tummy, if mum was smoking before or after birth, if the child is co-sleeping with a parent, or if she is allowed to become overheated, she is at greater risk of SIDS (taken from the NIH Safe to Sleep Public Education Campaign, www.nichd.nih.gov, and

NHS choices, www.nhs.uk). Because of the associated risk, parents are advised to always place infants on their back for sleeping.

Many parents wonder whether a young child who rolls onto her tummy in the night should be repositioned on her back. The National Institute of Child Health and Human Development (NICHD in the US) recommends that children should not be repositioned in the night, as rolling is a developmentally appropriate activity and should not be restricted. However, care should be taken to ensure that no loose clothing is present in the child's sleeping area. If you are feeling particularly anxious about your child overnight, some parents find it helpful to install a baby monitor that can track a baby's breathing. While these devices may help you to sleep better, it is important to note that these products are not medical devices. They should not be used in place of following the recommendations for lowering SIDS risk.

## The science of sleep

Young children spend a lot of time asleep. By the time they are three, they will have spent more of their life asleep than awake! We know it's important for things like immune function, emotional health and memory formation, but we still don't really understand why we do it. Perhaps sleep is restorative, or perhaps it is something left over from our evolutionary past (when it was safer to sleep in the dark than move, as we could not see our enemy).

There are two basic forms of sleep, REM and non-REM. In REM sleep we can see the eyes moving back and forth under the eyelids. We can also see muscle twitches or facial expressions, and we might even hear our children vocalising. It is often in REM sleep that we have our most vivid dreams.

Non-REM sleep consists of cycling through a number of stages in a predictable order. A child will first drift off into a transition stage, where she can easily be woken up, although she will be drowsy. In Stage 2, which is considered proper sleep, your child will have fewer body movements, in addition to slower breathing and heart rate. About half of a night's sleep will be spent in Stage 2, with the majority of this happening in the middle of the night.

Stages 3 and 4 are known as deep sleep, where we have slower and more regular heartbeat and breathing. While there is very little whole body movement in deep sleep, it is in these stages where sleep walking can occur. If woken in this stage, your child will be difficult to arouse and will be disoriented and confused. Most stage 3 and 4 sleep occurs towards the beginning of the night. Below is a hypnogram showing typical sleep patterns over a 24 hour period. The diagram makes clear the changes taking place from the ages of three months to two years.

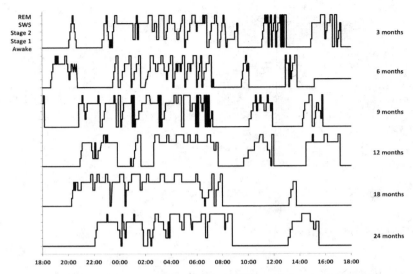

*Figure 2.1* 24 hour hypnograms for a typical child aged three to 24 months
(adapted with permission from Louis et al., 1997).

### Newborn sleep

At birth, the baby's biological clock is not well established. Her circadian
rhythms have not yet fully developed and she is just as likely to sleep in the
day as she is in the evening. If she is a typical full term newborn, sleep is
likely for around 16–18 hours each day, with the longest sleeps lasting
between 2.5 and 4 hours. Often sleeping will be coordinated with patterns
of feeding.

Similar to older children and adults, two main types of sleep are found in
the newborn, quiet sleep (non-REM sleep) and active or REM sleep. In quiet
sleep, she will not move much and has noticeably regular breathing. In
active sleep, she may suck, twitch, smile, frown, have irregular breathing
and may move her arms and legs. As an infant does not yet have a fully
developed block on her motor impulses, this is quite different from the
paralysis of REM sleep in older children. Infants also have shorter sleep
cycles than older children, and fall directly into REM sleep. They are also
more easily woken or disrupted.

## At what point will she start to sleep through the night?

When your child reaches two to three months, you may notice that her
circadian rhythms are becoming more established. Sleep is now likely to

be much more synchronised to the light cues outside, or even those in her bedroom. Feeding times and rituals will play an even more significant role in when, how often and how long your child sleeps. However, with a little bit of luck, it won't take long before your child is doing her longest sleeps at night (with a distinct morning and afternoon sleep).

By six months she (and you) may be enjoying up to six to eight hours of uninterrupted lovely night time sleep! So, if you put your child down at 8 in the evening, she may well sleep until 4 the next day. A long sleep over these hours is considered sleeping through the night. Alternatively, it is common at this stage for the night time period to consist of two long sleeps, with one feed in between. By the age of one, total sleep usually comes to 14 hours, including either one or two short naps during the day. As your child matures, she will need less sleep. By the age of two, a maximum of 13 hours is the norm, 12 hours by age three and 11 hours by age five (Davis, Parker and Montgomery, 2004). Naps are typically given up at around the age of three or four dependent upon the child.

---

### Parent post – co-sleeping

*I'm in the last few weeks of my pregnancy and I've been reading about co-sleeping and considering it as an option. I'm a bit confused though. Does the baby sleep in between you? Is there not a danger that the baby will get too warm or get caught under the duvet?*

---

Many parents consider co-sleeping (also known as bed sharing) with a new baby. However, expert advice suggests co-sleeping, where the baby shares the mother's bed, presents a higher risk of suffocation or strangulation, as well as SIDS. A popular alternative is to have a basinet/Moses basket next to the bed, or a cot with a dropdown side (sometimes called a co-sleeper). This means the baby can be easily accessed, but she has her own protected space. While a minority choose co-sleeping long term, many more parents will occasionally share a bed with an infant. Often this can be unintentional, as a tired parent falls asleep with a baby in her arms. Certain precautions should be taken where there is a possibility bed sharing may occur.

Some precautions for co-sleeping/bed sharing:

- Premature infants should not bed share.
- Bed sharing should not occur if anyone in the bed has taken medication, drugs or alcohol, or is excessively tired.
- Infants should always sleep on their back on firm surfaces, so no waterbeds, shaggy rugs, beanbags, sofas or duvets.

- Infants should not be put where they are in danger of slipping into a gap between a mattress and a wall.
- Infants should not be near pillows or stuffed animals.
- Infants should not have their heads covered, or be in danger of having their heads covered, with blankets or duvets or other things.
- Infants should not be in a room where someone has been smoking or share a bed with someone who has been smoking.
- Adults or children sleeping in the shared bed should be aware of the baby. Ideally, they should all agree to take responsibility for the baby's well-being. A baby should never be put into a bed where a sleeping adult or child does not know that she is there.

Research led information on baby sleep and bed sharing can be found on the Durham University ISIS (Infant Sleep Information Source), www.isisonline. org.uk.

## What are the pros and cons of co-sleeping/bed sharing?

### Pros

Easy breastfeeding is the main advantage of co-sleeping. Some mums find they can breastfeed without fully waking up, and it may also be less disruptive for the baby. Another plus is that baby and adult can be very near to each other. This may be very nice for both of you and may support bonding.

### Cons

The main cons of co-sleeping are the associated increased risk of suffocation, strangulation and sudden infant death syndrome (SIDS, see earlier discussion of risks and recommended precautions). Some research evidence also suggests co-sleeping infants may experience more stress than those sleeping separately (Hunsley & Thoman, 2002). You may also find co-sleeping uncomfortable, and some parents find that having a separate bed means they get more sleep.

## Sleep problems

Many children go through periods of disrupted or shortened sleep. In the UK, about one in five children under five will have serious difficulties either settling themselves to sleep or waking during the night (Ramchandani et al., 2000). When disrupted sleep is related to stressful events (problems in the parent relationship, job loss or periods of depression), it can be difficult for parents to know whether professional help is needed.

### How do I know if my child has a sleep problem?

GPs will tell you that lack of sleep is the most common complaint from parents of young children. Night time tussles and little rest can mean that life becomes more stressful, and it can be difficult to maintain enthusiasm for daily life. It's not only the night time awakenings but the impact they have on the next day, where everyone can be tired and cranky. A toddler who does not sleep well has a reduced ability to focus her attention and manage her emotions. This means her frustrations are amplified, she has more tantrums, more unreasonable behaviour, and little persistence with tasks. In sum, a well rested two year old is a much easier and more fun person to spend time with.

So when do sleep issues become problematic? A child's sleep is a problem if it is disrupting family life. Whether she is waking frequently during the night or getting up too early, if it is causing unhappiness to the rest of the family, then it is a problem. As a general guide, your child may be considered to have a sleep problem if she typically wakes more than five nights a week, wakes more than three times in one night, regularly takes more than 30 minutes to fall asleep, or requires mum or dad to be there to fall asleep.

---

### Parent post – bed wetting

*Our four year old is still wetting the bed every night. We've been keeping him in pull-ups, but recently, having spent some time with his cousins, he now refuses to wear one. This means that he is waking up at least once every night with wet sheets. We are all exhausted and pretty tired of wet bedding, so any advice would be very welcome!*

---

## What to do when your child is still wetting the bed

Night time bed wetting, which is clinically known as nocturnal enuresis, is common in children under five. Children do not wet the bed on purpose, so kindness and patience are always appropriate.

Bed wetting often occurs due to a mismatch between the size of a child's bladder and the amount of urine produced overnight. If your child is bed wetting, it may be that she is not sensitive to the feeling of a full bladder. Alternatively, she may be such a deep sleeper that she is not waking up enough to realise she needs the toilet. In some cases, children who are bed wetting may not be producing enough vasopressin, which is a hormone that lowers the production of urine overnight. In these cases medication can help.

For older children still wetting the bed, an alarm can be helpful. In this setup, a child has a moisture sensitive alarm placed into her pyjamas. When she starts to urinate, the buzzer or alarm goes off, waking her and allowing her to finish urinating in the toilet. When first getting used to this arrangement, the parent may need to wake the child. However, over time, she should learn to wake to the alarm, and then eventually wake herself to use the toilet without the alarm, or hold on until morning. The full process can take up to a few months to complete. However, alarm treatments demonstrate longer lasting effects than the drug treatment outlined above (Hunsley & Thoman, 2002). Lifting, where an adult lifts the child out of bed half asleep and regularly puts them on the toilet, is not recommended. This practice usually has only a short term impact and is not encouraged by medical practitioners.

In most typical children, physical maturation will solve any bed wetting issues. In the meantime, ensuring your child knows that wetting the bed is very common may help her to get back into a pull-up. Below are a few tips to manage bed wetting until the dry nights arrive.

### TIPS TO MANAGE BED WETTING

- Make sure your child uses the toilet before bed.
- Make sure she has easy access to the toilet at night (no restrictive pyjamas – i.e. no onesies – and no top bunk on a bunk bed).
- Rewards or incentive schemes for a dry bed are probably not appropriate as she likely cannot control the bed wetting.
- Use lots of positive encouragement.

### TIPS ON GOOD SLEEP TIME BEHAVIOURS FOR YOUNG CHILDREN

1   Consistent routines – evening meal, bath, storytime and bedtime should be at consistent times each day. Children should also get up at the same time each day to make sure they are getting a stable, consistent amount of sleep.
2   Be careful with caffeine and sugar – chocolate contains caffeine and you may wish to be thoughtful about how close to bedtime your children eat chocolate or other sugary snacks.
3   Limit active play or stimulating TV directly before bed. Children may find it difficult to settle themselves afterwards.
4   A darkened room can help many children to fall asleep, and also a room which is quiet and not too hot can help your child to settle.

5    Creating a cuddle routine, where your child gets some special one
     on one time, can help your child look forward to, and not resist, going
     to sleep.

## Frequently asked questions – sleep

### Do newborns dream?

Children as young as two can describe their dreams when woken from
REM sleep. However, younger children lack the language to communicate. We therefore cannot really know whether or not they dream, or
what these dreams might consist of. While it's clear that infants lack
the cognitive development to dream as we do, REM occurs from birth.
It's therefore not unreasonable to suggest that even infants dream.

### Do all children wake in the night?

We all wake, or come close to consciousness, as we cycle through
sleep episodes in the night. In young children, it is common for a child
to partially wake each night, usually at the end of a sleep cycle. Night
awakenings can occur as often as five to seven times per evening.
Usually, a child will have a look around the room and, if everything is
as expected, return to sleep within five minutes. It is for this reason that
experts advise parents to put children to bed when they are drowsy,
but not asleep. Encouraging your child to go off to sleep by herself
teaches self-soothing techniques that will be useful when she wakes
during the night.

### What are night terrors?

Sleep terrors occur when a child is in deep non-REM sleep, in the first
third of the night. Children partially wake up with confusion and, after
the age of four, often report having felt they were trying to escape or
outrun something. Parents see terrified expressions, mumbling,
shouting and children who are inconsolable. An underlying breathing
difficulty has been identified in some children suffering from night
terrors (Guilleminault et al., 2003). It is important to seek your GP's
assistance to discuss your child's individual case.

**What should I do if my child is sleepwalking?**

The most common treatment for children who are sleepwalking is to advise parents to provide a safe environment for their child. However, if there is a great concern for the safety of the child, perhaps she is letting herself out of the house in her night time wanderings, it may be that an intervention is needed. Scheduled awakenings involve waking the child three hours after she has gone to sleep and then just before she would typically sleepwalk. While the evidence is limited, studies have reported success with this type of treatment for both sleepwalking and night terrors (Frank et al., 1997).

**Do formula fed children sleep longer or better?**

Babies who are breastfed feed more frequently. This means they will have different sleep patterns from those of their formula fed counterparts. Some studies have shown that, on average, breastfed babies are slightly older when they first begin to sleep through the night and that they wake more frequently (Pinilla & Birch, 1993). The difference in behaviour lies in the nature of breast milk, which is very easy for the baby to digest compared to formula.

**Is co-sleeping dangerous?**

Whether intentionally or not, it is likely that we, as exhausted parents or carers, will at some point fall asleep with our babies in bed. In 2014, the National Institute for Health and Care Excellence (NICE) updated its guidance to clarify an association between co-sleeping and SIDS (available at www.nice.org.uk). Their guidelines now state that if a parent smokes, drinks alcohol or takes drugs, then SIDS is more likely to occur if the infant and parent are co-sleeping. The United Nations Children's Fund (UNICEF) has adapted these recommendations into a leaflet ('Caring for Your Baby at Night Time', www.unicef.org.uk) and advises that the safest place for a baby to sleep is in a cot next to the bed.

**Does sleeping longer/better mean my child will grow taller?**

Growth hormone is released while children sleep. For this reason, some parents may think that children who don't get a good night's sleep may be shorter than those who do. Studies investigating children with sleep problems have found a minor association with height. However, in the general population bodily growth and amount of time spent sleeping are not related (Jenni et al., 2007).

**What is colic?**

Colic is a condition in which a baby cries intensely for long periods in the first weeks after birth. A colicky baby will often have a bloated tummy, with legs sometimes pulled up, and may seem to feel better after a poo or relieving wind. For these reasons, it is often assumed that colic is caused by intestinal pain. However, it's also possible that the bloating may be caused by the child swallowing air during crying and that the underlying cause may be something different entirely. Often it is recommended that colicky infants be allowed a few bouts of crying, as they appear to benefit from the crying itself, without any particular remedy required. Colic appears to be most severe during the evenings. The condition normally clears up by itself around the age of three months.

**My child's poor sleeping is affecting the whole family, is there anything I can do?**

While it is always a good idea to discuss sleep issues with your GP, there are now additional sources of help available. For example, apps for mobile devices are available which can help you to record the sleep patterns of your child. The best of these have been developed in collaboration with medical doctors and will assess the inputted sleep patterns in order to offer appropriate advice.

**I'm really worried, my two month old's head is really flat on one side. She always sleeps with her head to the left. What should I do?**

In most cases, a flattened head is no cause for concern. It is quite typical for babies, who spend much of their time on their backs. There are two types, flattening at the back of the head, known as brachy-cephaly, and flattening on the side of the head, known as plagiocephaly.

When the side is flattened, the head will appear asymmetrical, and one of your child's ears may be misaligned. When the back is flattened, your baby's head may widen, and in some cases the forehead may bulge.

Head flattening is particularly common in premature babies. Infants who have not reached full term often have very soft skulls and underdeveloped neck muscles and neck movement. However, parents should not worry; a flattened head will not affect the development of the brain. In most cases, your baby's head shape will become more rounded over time. Also, as your child becomes a toddler and hair grows, a slight flattening will no longer be visible.

While head flattening is usually nothing serious, it is advisable to have a professional check your baby's skull. Often you will be given exercises to do together and will be encouraged to frequently place your baby on her tummy. It may also be recommended that you carry her in a sling, and occasionally place her in a sloping chair. Using these techniques will alleviate the pressure on your baby's head.

Where head flattening is severe, helmets are available. These are placed on an infant when she is six months old or under, and worn almost continuously for several months. The idea is that the helmet puts pressure on the areas of the skull that are bulging, while allowing other areas to grow. While the wearing of helmets has been shown to normalise head shape, it is not clear that they are more effective than using the techniques outlined above (Van Vlimmeren et al., 2006). Certainly, the cost, inconvenience and discomfort should be considered before deciding on using a helmet with your baby.

## References

Davis, K. F., Parker, K. P., & Montgomery, G. L. (2004). Sleep in infants and young children. *Journal of Pediatric Health Care, 18*(2), 65–71.

Ferber, R. (1985). *Solve Your Child's Sleep Problems*. New York, NY: Simon & Schuster.

Frank, N. C., Spirito, A., Stark, L., & Owens-Stively, J. (1997). The use of scheduled awakenings to eliminate childhood sleepwalking. *Journal of Pediatric Psychology, 22*(3), 345–353.

Guilleminault, C., Biol, D., Palombini, L., Pelayo, R., & Chervin, R. D. (2003). Sleepwalking and sleep terrors in prepubertal children: What triggers them? *Pediatrics, 111*, e17–e25.

Hiscock, H., & Wake, M. (2002). Randomised controlled trial of behavioural infant sleep intervention to improve infant sleep and maternal mood. *BMJ, 324*(May), 1–6.

Hunsley, M., & Thoman, E. B. (2002). The sleep of co-sleeping infants when they are not co-sleeping: Evidence that co-sleeping is stressful. *Developmental Psychobiology, 40*(1), 14–22. http://doi.org/10.1002/dev.10009

Jenni, O. G., Molinari, L., Caflisch, J., & Largo, R. H. (2007). Sleep duration from ages 1 to 10 years: variability and stability in comparison with growth. *Pediatrics, 120*(4), e769-776. http://doi.org/10.1542/peds.2006-3300

Louis, J., Cannard, C., Bastuji, H., & Challamel, M.-J. J. (1997). Sleep ontogenesis revisited: A longitudinal 24-hour home polygraphic study on 15 normal infants during the first two years of life. *Sleep, 20*(5), 323–333.

Pavlov, I. P. (1927). Conditioned reflexes: An investigation of the physiological activity of the cerebral cortex. *Annals of Neurosciences.* http://doi.org/10.5214/ans.0972-7531.1017309

Pinilla, T., & Birch, L. (1993). Help me make it through the night: Behavioral entrainment of breast-fed infants' sleep patterns. *Pediatrics, 91*, 436.

Price, A. M. H., Wake, M., Ukoumunne, O. C., & Hiscock, H. (2012). Five-year follow-up of harms and benefits of behavioral infant sleep intervention: Randomized trial. *Pediatrics, 130*(4), 643–651. http://doi.org/10.1542/peds.2011-3467

Ramchandani, P., Wiggs, L., Webb, V., & Stores, G. (2000). A systematic review of treatments for settling problems and night waking in young children. *BMJ (Clinical Research Ed.), 320*(7229), 209–13.

Van Vlimmeren, L. A., Helders, P. J. M., Van Adrichem, L. N. A., & Engelbert, R. H. H. (2006). Torticollis and plagiocephaly in infancy: Therapeutic strategies. *Pediatric Rehabilitation, 9*(1), 40–46. http://doi.org/10.1080/13638490500037904

Becky Cameron

# 3   What's the truth on breast versus bottle?

## Parent post – breastfeeding

*I am so fed up with breastfeeding! It's just not working for me. I've struggled with it from day one. Either I'm not producing enough milk, or she's not getting it, I don't know which. Whatever's happening, she's always screaming and I'm exhausted, and my nipples are incredibly sore! I've seen every lactating and breastfeeding expert going. They've been round to the house, helping me to position the baby properly, and making sure we get skin to skin contact. To be honest, it's stressful, and the breastfeeding's not getting any better. I can't see any other option, I'm going to start with formula. While I was pregnant, I was really keen on the idea of exclusive breastfeeding. Now I feel like such a failure. Everything I read says how great breastfeeding is for babies. Have I let my daughter down by not giving her the best start in life?*

Breastfeeding is an emotional topic. Many mums and dads (or grannies and grandpas, doctors, midwives or even strangers with no children) have strong views and aren't afraid to share them with you. Women are told again and again that breast is best, so it's not surprising we feel the pressure to nurse, no matter what our personal opinions may be.

While many women will have a wonderful, easy time breastfeeding their babies, things can get stressful when feeding a baby doesn't go to plan. For some women, the reality of breastfeeding falls drastically short of any pre-baby ideals. For these mums, breastfeeding is not a joyous bonding experience, it is filled with stress, exhaustion, guilt, worry and sometimes pain (with sore breasts and cracked and chafed nipples).

## Making the choice between breast and formula feeding

So how do we know what choice to make for a positive and successful feeding experience? Breast milk is a nutritious, perfect food for an infant, and breastfeeding can be a wonderful shared experience. However, any expert worth her salt will tell you that feeding choices are personal and should be made by the family, not healthcare professionals. The full set of factors needs to be weighed up. If getting a breastfeeding routine going is causing you serious problems, calmly review the situation. Is your baby putting on the appropriate weight? Is the family suffering (anxiety/exhaustion) from the current feeding arrangements? How would continuing with breastfeeding, versus supplementing with formula, impact upon you, the baby and the family over the next few weeks and months?

With these thoughts in mind, take the anxiety and guilt away, and remember that this is just one decision. There will be opportunities to make many important choices over the lifetime of your child. A child's development is shaped by a complex interplay of genes and the environment. The science suggests that our decisions on breastfeeding are not particularly related to who our child becomes. In families where one child is breastfed and one child is formula fed, there are no consistent differences between the two (Colen & Ramey, 2014).

## The science of infant feeding

### *Breast and formula feeding in recent history*

Breastfeeding has been the norm throughout history. So has the wet nurse. A wet nurse is a lactating woman who can feed the baby when mum can't, or doesn't want to. For a long time, wet nursing provided the only safe alternative to breastfeeding. However, since the early 1900s, alternatives have been available. It was around this time that the widespread availability of iceboxes and canned evaporated milk allowed relatively safe formula to be made at home. By the 1950s, commercial formulas were widely available and doctors began recommending them to supplement four hourly feeds when the baby appeared hungry. A decade later and the number of breastfeeding mothers was much lower, with the 1960s marking a worldwide low for breastfeeding (Hoddinott, Tappin, & Wright, 2008). It was also in this period that the composition of breast milk was more fully understood. While formulas evolved in an attempt to copy the proteins, fat and carbohydrates, breast milk remained a superior food for infants, providing the nursing child with immunological benefits. Breast milk has since been declared to be the optimal food for infants by the World Health Organisation

(WHO) and United Nations Children's Fund (UNICEF; UNICEF, UNAIDS, & WHO, 2003). The NHS recommends exclusive breastfeeding for the first six months, as does the American Academy of Pediatrics and the World Health Organisation.

## What exactly is infant formula?

Infant formula is prepared for bottle (or cup) feeding and is sold as a powder or concentrated liquid (both of which need water to be added), or in a ready to use format. Most formulas are prepared from cow's milk proteins, which have been altered to resemble breast milk. These formulas contain lactose and minerals from the milk as well as a blend of vegetable oils and vitamins. Alternative formulas using soy proteins, which do not contain lactose, are available.

Formula is a highly regulated food and any changes must be extensively tested. Within the last few decades, a few alterations have been made. These have attempted to make formula closer to breast milk, and to increase health benefits. For example, some formulas have been fortified with iron, added nucleotides (a compound forming the basic structure of nucleic acids such as DNA) and changed the composition of fat blends. In the US, discussions are under way to include genetically engineered compounds and probiotics in infant formulas (Committee on the Evaluation of the Addition of Ingredients New to Infant Formula, 2004).

## What does breast milk do that formula can't?

Breast milk is a unique food and, unlike formula, it changes over the course of the day and also as your baby develops. Over the first month, there are three distinct phases of breast milk; colostrum, transitional milk and mature milk. In the first days of breastfeeding, colostrum is full of antibodies, minerals and vitamins, supporting the development of the immune system. It is low in fat and carbohydrates and is yellow in colour, due to the high levels of vitamin A. Colostrum is very concentrated, and there's not much of it. From day two to four, milk is produced in larger amounts, usually making the breasts feel full. Over the first week, the levels of fat and lactose grow, and the protein, vitamin and mineral content decreases. This milk is called transitional and lasts up until day 14. In week three, mature milk is produced, which is one third foremilk and two thirds hindmilk. Fat is deposited in small drops in breastmilk, and the percentage of fat generally increases over the course of a feed. The hindmilk at the end of a feed appears creamy and white, while the foremilk at the beginning is bluish grey, similar to skimmed milk.

---

**Parent post – does breastfeeding
make your kid smarter?**

*I've just seen another news report telling us that breastfed babies are
more intelligent. I have four children, two I breastfed and two I bottle
fed with formula. They are all doing very well in their various stages
of education. I find it hard to believe that breastfeeding makes your
kids smart. Isn't intelligence based on genes? Bright parents have
bright kids, right?*

---

## The problems of breastfeeding research

So much time and effort has been spent on testing the impact of breastfeeding. But this research is very problematic. The 'breast is best' campaign
suggests breastfeeding our children will make them brighter, healthier and
more bonded to us. There is lots of vested interest in demonstrating better
outcomes for breastfed babies.

However, the problem is this. In order to test any impact of breastfeeding
on babies, let's say we want to test whether breastfed babies are smarter,
we would need to randomly assign a feeding method. So we would need
to select a representation of the population and then tell some mothers to
breastfeed and some mothers to use formula. Of course, we usually can't
do this for ethical reasons. Breastfeeding for full term babies is not a medical
intervention, and usually we have no ethical grounds for undertaking such a
study. So, we therefore have to use groups that already exist. So, for example,
researchers assess the cognitive development of a group of children who are
breastfed. They then compare their outcomes to a group of children who
are formula fed, and assess the differences.

### No clear long term differences between breast and formula fed babies

Using naturally occurring groups (as described above) has been very common
in breastfeeding research. Studies published since the early 1990s have
consistently found that children who are breastfed have higher IQs than those
who are formula fed. These experiments are very unreliable. Breast and
bottle fed babies also differ in lots of other ways. Breastfeeding in first world
countries is tied to maternal education, socio-economic class and ethnicity
(Li et al., 2005). So, in other words, children who are breastfed are more
likely to have many education-related advantages compared to formula fed

children. Studies that compare the two groups are not comparing like with like. When differences are found, they could easily be explained by breastfed children having more social advantages (such as access to books, rich cultural experiences and a stimulating home environment) or a genetic inheritance which supports intellectual development.

A few more recent studies have used a sibling design. This works by finding families where one baby was formula fed, and the other baby was breastfed. A comparison of sibling outcomes provides some control for genes (on average 50% of DNA) and shared environment (home, parenting, etc.). Interestingly, no differences in IQ have been found using this design (Der, Batty, & Deary, 2006). An additional sibling study, comparing breast and formula fed children, found no differences between the groups on measures of obesity, asthma, hyperactivity, attachment, intelligence or any of the other areas measured (Colen & Ramey, 2014).

Confirmatory evidence has been found in an additional unique study. In this research, a randomly chosen group of mothers in Belarus was given breastfeeding support. While the mothers attending the sessions were more likely to take up breastfeeding, their children experienced no reduction in asthma or allergies, dental cavities or problem behaviour, compared to the non-breastfeeding group (Kramer, Chalmers, & Hodnett, 2001).

---

### Parent post – milk supply difficulties

*I am currently pregnant with my second child. I had almost no success breastfeeding my first. I tried everything, including pumping, but my boy wasn't doing well, so eventually he was given formula and the milk dried up soon after. Since then, my doctor has told me that I might be low on ductile tissue. It might be that I just wasn't able to make an adequate amount of breast milk to feed my baby. However, I remember the breastfeeding expert at the time telling me that all women produce more than enough milk to feed their babies. She said that when babies are slow to gain weight, this is because the baby does not get the milk that the mother has, usually because of a poor latch onto the breast. I'm really sure my problems weren't down to the latch. Everyone I saw told me I was doing it right. I just don't know what to think. I want to have reasonable expectations with the birth of my second. Is it the case that some women simply can't breastfeed or was I just not doing it right?*

## Milk supply difficulties in breastfeeding

While most sources will tell you that all women can breastfeed, some medical reports suggest there are a small number of women who have biological reasons for low milk supply. In one example, women requiring formula to supplement their babies' diets were found to have insufficient glandular development (Neifert, Seacat, & Jobe, 1985). While pumping and drinking water may help, maintaining exclusive breastfeeding may be more challenging for these women. Unfortunately, the underlying causes are not well understood. However, we do know that women who have had breast surgery (whether cosmetic or medical), have low thyroid hormone, have polycystic ovary syndrome (PCOS) or pituitary problems or have experienced excessive haemorrhaging after birth, may face difficulties with low milk supply (Marasco, Marmet, & Shell, 2000). The stress of a long labour or emergency Caesarean section may also be related to difficulties in milk production and establishing breastfeeding (Dewey, 2001). For these women, stress may be getting in the way of oxytocin release, which is then impairing the flow of milk from the breast, and over time lowering the level of milk production.

## Why do mothers stop breastfeeding?

It makes sense that in order to want to continue breastfeeding long term (six months and beyond), both baby and mother must be enjoying the experience. Mothers who feel their babies are well nourished by their feeds, sleep well and appear settled and happy to play between feeds are more likely to continue long term. Mums who stop after a month to six weeks provide a few common explanations, including sore nipples, inadequate milk supply, difficulties with the baby's development, the feeling that the baby is not getting enough nourishment, returning to work and sharing feeding responsibilities with dad or another adult. Mums who are experiencing depression, either since the birth of the baby or as a longer term condition, are also more likely to stop breastfeeding soon after giving birth (Henderson et al., 2003).

---

### Parent post – breastfeeding at work

*I've been exclusively breastfeeding my baby for the past two months, but now I need to return to work part-time. While my department is really friendly, I don't think they have any particular support for breastfeeding mothers. I need some advice on how to speak to them about supporting me in continuing to breastfeed my little girl.*

## Going back to work while breastfeeding

Many mums would like to continue breastfeeding after returning to work. To make this happen, some find it easiest to arrange childcare that is close to work, so that breastfeeding can take place during breaks and before and after work. Alternatively, expressing milk either by hand or using a pump can give you freedom during the day, while allowing your child to continue receiving your breast milk. Either way you are likely to need to talk to your employer. In the UK, the government advises providing your employer with a letter stating that you are returning to work and continuing to breastfeed. Your employer must then undertake a risk assessment and provide a suitable place where you can rest when needed. The Health and Safety Executive also recommends that a workplace provide a private, healthy and safe environment for breastfeeding mothers to express and store milk (not the toilets).

### Frequently asked questions – breastfeeding

**Are there particular foods that a breastfeeding mum should eat?**

There is currently very little evidence to show a link between what a mum eats, the composition of her breast milk and her child's development (Innis, 2014). The overall fat, lactose and protein content of your milk is unaffected by your diet. This is largely the same for the mineral content, although diet can impact upon iodine levels in your milk. There are a few vitamins that vary in breast milk in relation to the mother's diet; these are vitamin A, vitamin B-6 and vitamin B-12, amongst others (Innis, 2014).

**Should I breastfeed/feed my child on demand (also known as baby-led feeding)?**

A number of parenting books advocate using a schedule to feed your baby, and an equal number praise baby led feeding. Scientific research has little to add to this debate. Ethically, it is not possible to assign breastfeeding behaviours to groups of mums and therefore we cannot draw any conclusions regarding either method.

Most health organisations recommend baby led feeding. This is due to a number of factors. (1) If your baby is left to cry and becomes agitated, she may have difficulty calming herself to feed subsequently. (2) Babies have differences in their efficiency in getting milk from the breast; yours may need frequent opportunities to get her fill. (3) The mother's breast needs to be stimulated frequently in order to produce new milk and you may not be producing the same quantities of milk for all feeds. (4) Sensitive responding to your baby helps to promote a secure attachment.

Like most parenting issues, the correct approach is the one that fits you, your baby and the rest of your family. Hearing the experiences of family members and friends can be helpful, but ultimately you need to get to know your baby and, after a bit of trial and error, find what works for you.

### I have heard that breast milk protects my newborn against getting sick as it pumps up her immune system. Is this true?

Breast milk contains an antibody that can protect mucous membranes such as the digestive tract and the respiratory tract from bacteria and viruses. This means that breastfed babies are less likely to have diarrhoea or colds in their first year (Hoddinott, Tappin, & Wright, 2008). Large scale studies suggest that these protective properties disappear shortly after breastfeeding is stopped (Quigley, Kelly, & Sacker, 2007).

### Does breastfeeding protect infants from ear infections?

While some studies have shown a reduced risk for infants who were breastfed (for any amount of time), compared with infants who were formula fed, these studies did not control for confounding factors and are therefore unreliable (Hoddinott, Tappin, & Wright, 2008). There is currently no rigorous evidence for breastfeeding acting as a protection against ear infections.

### Does breast milk help infants to sleep?

While there are sleep-promoting compounds (melatonin) in breast milk produced at night, these may be related to the tiredness of the mother. Whether or not these components promote sleep in infants is unknown. It is thought to be unlikely as there is no evidence suggesting breastfed babies sleep longer than formula fed babies.

### I have heard that even one bottle of formula can undo the benefits of breastfeeding my baby. Is this true?

There have been some claims by strong proponents of breastfeeding that even one bottle of formula will have negative effects on your baby's gut microbiome. At present, there does not appear to be any substantial evidence supporting this claim. There is, however, evidence that small amounts of formula can help to establish breastfeeding when the baby is losing weight or while the mother's milk is coming in (Flaherman et al., 2013). This means that when a new baby is not making appropriate weight gain, formula can provide an effective supplemental nutrition and does not mean the mother cannot breastfeed.

### Due to the medication I am taking, I am not able to breastfeed my baby. Will I feel less bonded to my baby because I'm not breastfeeding her?

Breastfeeding is thought to promote a bond between mother and infant through the release of oxytocin. In the process of nursing, a surge of oxytocin is released which may promote feelings of closeness, protectiveness and love between mother and baby. However, this does not mean that in non-breastfeeding relationships the mother and baby will not be bonded.

Recent studies suggest that while breastfeeding may facilitate early bonding, bottle feeding is also related to high quality mother–infant relationships, particularly around the one year mark (Matthiesen et al., 2001).

### What are oxytocin and prolactin and why are they important?

Prolactin is a hormone necessary for milk secretion; it is released from the pituitary gland and controlled by the hypothalamus. Prolactin levels increase over pregnancy and peak at birth, from which point they gradually decrease. Progesterone and oestrogen block the prolactin during pregnancy, but after delivery these hormones drop quickly and milk secretion begins. When a baby suckles at the breast, the level of prolactin increases, stimulating milk production. During the first few weeks, the more the baby suckles, the more prolactin and milk are produced. This relationship may be particularly important in establishing lactation in the first few weeks.

Oxytocin is another hormone produced by the hypothalamus and released by the pituitary. It is related to feelings of closeness and bonding and plays a role in sexual relations. It is also key in bringing on the increasing contractions of labour. Oxytocin is released in response to the baby suckling at the breast, or in anticipation of a feed. It triggers the let down of milk which is already stored in the breast. Often mothers can feel a tingling sensation related to the milk ejection reflex.

**How many mothers are breastfeeding their babies these days?**

Breastfeeding has had its ups and downs in popularity. Currently, under half of all mothers are breastfeeding at two months (44% at least partially breastfeeding; Public Health England, 2016); in the US the proportion is slightly higher (Centers for Disease Control and Prevention, 2014).

## Resources

Centers for Disease Control and Prevention. (2014). Breastfeeding Report Card, United States. Available at www.cdc.gov

Colen, C., & Ramey, D. (2014). Is breast truly best? Estimating the effect of breast-feeding on long-term wellbeing in the United States using sibling comparisons. *Social Science & Medicine*, *109*, 55–65. http://doi.org/10.1016/j.socscimed.2014.01.027.Is

Der, G., Batty, G. D., & Deary, I. J. (2006). Effect of breast feeding on intelligence in children: Prospective study, sibling pairs analysis, and meta-analysis. *BMJ*, *55*(October). http://doi.org/10.1136/bmj.38978.699583.55

Dewey, K. G. (2001). Maternal and fetal stress are associated with impaired lactogenesis in humans. *Journal of Nutrition*, *131*(11), 3012S–3015S.

Flaherman, V., Aby, J., Burgos, A. E., Lee, K. A., Cabana, M. D., & Newman, T. (2013). Effect of early limited formula on duration and exclusivity of breast-feeding in at-risk infants: An RCT. *Pediatrics*, *131*(6), 1059–1065. http://doi.org/10.1542/peds.2012-2809

Henderson, J. J., Evans, S. F., Straton, J. A. Y., Priest, S. R., & Hagan, R. (2003). Impact of postnatal depression on breastfeeding duration [corrected] [published erratum appears in *Birth* (2004) March, *31*(1): 76]. *Birth: Issues in Perinatal Care*, *30*(September), 175–180. http://doi.org/10.1046/j.1523-536X.2003.00242.x

Hoddinott, P., Tappin, D., & Wright, C. (2008). Breast feeding. *British Medical Journal*, (April), 881–887. http://doi.org/10.1136/bmj.39521.566296.BE

Innis, S. M. (2014). Impact of maternal diet on human milk composition and neurological development of infants. *American Journal of Clinical Nutrition*, *99*, 734–741. http://doi.org/10.3945/ajcn.113.072595.734S

Institute of Medicine (US), Committee on the Evaluation of the Addition of Ingredients New to Infant Formula. (2004). *Infant Formula: Evaluating the Safety of New Ingredients.* Washington, DC: National Academies Press.

Kramer, M. S., Chalmers, B., & Hodnett, E. D. (2001). Promotion of breastfeeding intervention trial (PROBIT): A randomized trial in the Republic of Belarus. *Journal of the American Medical Association, 285*(4), 413–420. http://doi.org/10.1001/jama.285.4.413

Li, R., Darling, N., Maurice, E., Barker, L., & Grummer-Strawn, L. (2005). Breastfeeding rates in the United States by characteristics of the child, mother, or family: The 2002 National Immunization Survey. *Pediatrics, 115*(1), e31–e37.

Marasco, L., Marmet, C., & Shell, E. (2000). Polycystic ovary syndrome: A connection to insufficient milk supply? *Journal of Human Lactation, 16*(2), 143–148. http://doi.org/10.1177/089033440001600211

Matthiesen, A. S., Ransjö-Arvidson, A. B., Nissen, E., & Uvnäs-Moberg, K. (2001). Postpartum maternal oxytocin release by newborns: Effects of infant hand massage and sucking. *Birth (Berkeley, Calif.), 28*(1), 13–19.

Neifert, M., Seacat, J., & Jobe, W. (1985). Lactation failure due to glandular development. *Pediatrics, 76*(5), 823–828.

Public Health England. (2016). Official statistics: Breastfeeding prevelance at 6–8 weeks after birth (experimental statistics). 2016/17 Quarter 3. Available at www.gov.uk

Quigley, M. A., Kelly, Y. J., & Sacker, A. (2007). Breastfeeding and hospitalization for diarrheal and respiratory infection in the United Kingdom Millennium Cohort Study. *Pediatrics, 119*(4), e837–e842.

UNICEF, UNAIDS, & WHO. (2003). *HIV and infant feeding guidelines for decision-makers.* Geneva: World Health Organisation.

Becky Cameron

# 4 How much is too much screen time?

---

**Parent post – limiting screen time**

*I get that watching unlimited TV can't be good for kids. But I struggle with what to do about screen time. I'm a screen lover. I am constantly on my phone, ipad or laptop. It seems obvious to me that my children should love it too. Limiting screen time doesn't come naturally to me. So, let's say, I impose a maximum of two hours' screen time each day. How does that work? Does looking at a book on an e-reader, or using an early literacy app, count the same as watching a cartoon? That doesn't make sense to me. I need a reasonable approach that works for my family.*

---

Today's parents can't avoid the topic of screens. There are some difficult decisions to be made. How, when, what and for how long should our children access and interact with digital and online content?

Mobile phones and digital/video media are a part of our children's everyday lives. Once they enter school, interacting with these technologies is guaranteed, as is the frequent use of computers, tablets and maybe even games consoles. We, as parents, can encourage good media habits right from the start. This includes setting clear limits.

The best known guidance on screen time comes from the American Academy of Pediatrics. Through their Media Matters (1997) campaign and policy statements (e.g. American Academy of Pediatrics, Committee on Public Education, 2001) they have publicised the $2 \times 2$ rule: no screens for under twos, and a maximum of two hours of screen time per day for children two and above.

Developed when TVs were the only screen on offer, this guidance has long been out of date. Our under twos are now frequently found using touch tablets and phones to view and play with digital content. In fact, companies actively develop content to appeal to the under two market and their parents. Early learning apps and games, as well as nursery video portals, are very popular. But under twos are not only accessing age appropriate material; they also do a lot of watching with older siblings. All of this adds up to reports of two and unders in the US watching more than an hour and a half of television per day (Zimmerman, Christakis, & Meltzoff, 2007).

## American Academy of Pediatrics' (AAP) screen time guidance

Under pressure to update its guidelines, the American Academy of Pediatrics has recently issued new advice on screen time (American Academy of Pediatrics, 2016). Gone is the complete ban on media for under twos. Viewing of high quality programming for one and a half to two year olds is now allowed, provided it takes place with an adult. However, the blanket time limit on all forms of screen media remains. For two to fives, a maximum of one hour of high quality screen time is advised. Video chatting is fine for all ages.

Many parents may rightly wonder why it is one hour in particular which is the maximum. Unfortunately, it's not clear. The AAP claims the new policy is based on scientific research. However, the research base for this particular choice is not evident. Again, it is miles away from the reality of many families.

## How to approach screen time (in your own way)

The goal of this book is to respond to parenting problems with research led options. When it comes to screen time, the approach that is going to work best is the one that fits your family. You may decide to impose a daily time limit on some, or all, screen media. Alternatively, you may like to be more flexible and make your decisions on a daily basis. If you feel uncertain about making choices, being clear on the areas of concern may help. The research which highlights an importance for limiting screen time is presented below. Associated guidance that emerges from the research follows each section.

### *Research areas highlighting concerns on children and screen media*

#### *Learning*

Children aged two and under do not learn as well from digital media as they do from us. For example, nursery DVDs are not effective in teaching new words (Robb, Richert, & Wartella, 2009). Children may also not fully benefit from e-books and may have a poorer understanding of the story and reduced vocabulary development than when using traditional paper based storybooks (Bus, Takacs, & Kegel, 2015).

**Associated guidance (learning)**

1   Because digital content cannot replace chatting together, plenty of time and opportunity should be made for your child to undertake routines where language learning can flourish. Examples are cooking dinner, doing the washing, getting ready for bed, etc. When these times of the day are screen free, both of you can make the most of your time together.
2   Where possible, sit with your child and interact with the game or programme together. Under twos have difficulty applying the 2D screen to the 3D world (Moser et al., 2015). It is therefore helpful to discuss the programming and relate it to the world around you. If you want to use your child's screen time to complete other tasks, then after the screen time has finished, you could ask some questions about what she's just seen. This can help to underline the learning of new words and concepts.
3   Make time for books. While e-books are great, non-interactive traditional books also have an important place in a child's life.

*BMI*

Excessive TV or screen time has consistently been linked with obesity. Even in young children, preschoolers who watch more TV have a higher body mass index (BMI). This higher body mass is most often assumed to be due to low activity levels. However, TV watching can also be associated with higher calorie consumption, for example when an older child (aged 9–14) watches TV when eating a meal. In this case, TV may be disrupting the cues a child normally associates with feeling full (Bellissimo et al., 2007).

**Associated guidance (BMI)**

1   Good amounts of physical activity and time outdoors interacting with the natural environment should be encouraged.
2   Children should not be watching TV or other digital media at mealtimes.

*Sleep*

Infants (12 month olds) who view digital programming before bed get less sleep (Moser et al., 2015), as do older children (aged three to five years) who have a television in their room (Garrison, Liekweg, & Christakis, 2011). In this study, children with a TV in their bedroom were also more likely to view violent content and have associated sleep difficulties.

## Associated guidance (sleep)

1   Avoid allowing your child to access digital content in the hour before bedtime.
2   It is recommended that a child not have a TV in her bedroom.

## Why are parents concerned about screens?

If you take a look around parenting forums online, you'll no doubt come across the topic of screen time. Today's parents have seen a big move from traditional media, such as books and radio, to the pervasive nature of screen based technologies. Mobile and touch based digital technologies have entered our lives at an amazing pace. For example, tablet computers, introduced in 2010, can now be found in over 65 per cent of UK homes (Ofcom, 2014).

Many parents are overwhelmed by how quickly everything has moved online, particularly the new modes of communication offered by social media. Some parents see their children continually using apps that they don't understand and know very little about. It is very reasonable to be concerned that some of this talk, sharing of photos or internet content may be inappropriate. Parents can feel powerless when it comes to setting boundaries, particularly when they do not know how to use or enforce the parental controls offered by the technology. Furthermore, when so many areas of a child's life, both for study and for socialising, take place online, screen time can become an area for heated and complicated debate. This is particularly the case for parents of older children.

While internet usage and mobile apps are quickly gaining in prominence, most parents of young children are still primarily concerned about TV. Although hours spent watching television are in fact slowly decreasing (likely replaced by watching similar content on mobile devices), some estimates in the US suggest preschoolers watch on average 4.4 hours of television per day (Christakis & Michelle, 2013). In the UK, it seems to be closer to around 2.5 hours. Although touch based technology is everywhere, young children can still most easily access the TV screen. TV is also the technology that is most commonly a standard part of a parenting routine. Parents often report using TV as a safe activity for children while things are done in the house, whether it is preparing dinner or getting ready to go out of the house. For this reason, parents can have a guilt association with TV. They can feel they are 'parking' their child in front of the TV, in order to get other things done.

## Are screens changing my child's brain?

Parents' concerns around screen time often centre around brain development. For example, parents are concerned that their child's brain will be 'wired differently' because 'she spends so much more time on screens than we ever did'. In fact, all learning affects the brain, as this is the essence of what learning is! Connections between frequently firing neurons in the brain form pathways that allow us to gain from our experiences and learn. While we are all looking at a lit screen more regularly, our brains will adapt to this, as they have consistently adapted to our use of cultural tools – such as the book. The use of a screen in and of itself is not intrinsically negative. The key is in the content and achieving a balance of learning through other media and getting involved in complimentary activities.

## How do children use digital media?

Children's media use differs depending upon age. By the time your child goes to secondary school, she will be using digital media quite flexibly. Much of this will involve communicating with her friends and will most likely include social networking sites and applications.

In young children, the relationship with digital technology is much more structured and controlled, particularly in preschoolers. Population studies (e.g. Ofcom, 2016) show young children use mobile technology to play with educational apps, either through games or watching videos. Reports suggest that three quarters of children aged six months to three years use a touchscreen on a daily basis, with an average usage time of 45 minutes per day for two to three year olds (Cheung et al., 2017). In many cases, the same digital content that was once watched on television is now watched through alternative means. For example, internet linked television allows programmes to be viewed on-demand, as do applications on mobile tablets and phones. Therefore, many of the concerns expressed about TV are very relevant to digital media.

## Kids and videos/TV

The under two media market is big business! Just look at the success of *Baby Einstein* and *Teletubbies*. While it used to be thought that young children had little, or only a fleeting, interest in television, we can no longer assume this to be the case. Baby led content means that young children can now show long periods of focused attention. This is likely due to the rapidly changing pictures and sounds, or it may be related to the simplified message conveyed. Experiments show that on average, by one year of age, children can pick up information from a video. For example, if an adult on TV appears afraid or happy about an object, infants will show similar emotions when shown the object in real life (Mumme & Fernald, 2003). Despite these and similar findings, the consensus is that the educational impact of baby DVDs is limited. Additionally, there has been some concern that time spent watching videos or TV is displacing face to face interaction, the ideal means through which infants develop language (Christakis et al., 2009).

### Does TV and video influence behaviour?

At around age three, children with access to television/video content become much more active viewers. Their linguistic and cognitive processing now allows for greater understanding of the programming, and children start to have strong ideas about what they want to watch!

Parents and researchers are keen to know the effects of TV watching, particularly whether violent content can cause aggressive behaviour in children. Many researchers suggest this may be the case and offer a number of explanations as to how it may occur. One possibility is that children's inhibitions may be lowered or that they may have their mood aroused by watching violence on TV. Another suggests that children are in a more negative mood after watching violent content and this impacts upon their subsequent behaviour.

Famous work on social learning theory by Albert Bandura suggests that children can learn aggressive behaviour simply by watching others. There have been other suggestions that watching violent content can have a long term impact of lowering sensitivity to violent behaviour and create more acceptance for violence. Some parents have argued that if violence is so silly that it couldn't happen in reality (picture kicking someone's head so that it rotates round and round), children can't copy it in their behaviour. However, researchers argue that viewing violence on TV can encourage disinhibition. In this scenario, a child feels more freedom to use the aggressive behaviours already in her repertoire such as hitting and pushing. In one randomised controlled trial, when aggressive content was switched to high quality, pro-social educational content, preschoolers showed more socially acceptable behaviours (Christakis & Michelle, 2013).

## How children learn using computers

Using computers offers children a unique opportunity for learning. In the early years, children learn to use technologies by watching others and by trying things out for themselves. In this way, young children gain *operational skills* such as how to use the mouse, touch screen or games controller, while familiarising themselves with a computer interface. Children can also increase their *knowledge of the world* and *means of creative expression*. The first most often takes place when *actively* engaging with software, a feature not always observed in children's play with technology. For preschoolers, computer software often promotes school readiness and aims to build familiarity with letters and numbers and other school related curriculum. The most common creative activities for young children involve taking photographs, using paint or art applications or making videos.

Computer use has also been linked to increasing a child's *disposition to learn*. This means encouraging socio-emotional development through boosting self-esteem and confidence in one's abilities. Such qualities can be encouraged through experiencing success in undertaking a task, particularly when using exciting new technologies. In addition to the above, children may also gain knowledge of the role of technology in our modern society. For example, preschoolers can learn how we may *communicate using technology*, using text based messaging systems or video calling, etc. These forms of communication will be central to interacting in their future social networks.

## Touch technology – children with tablets and mobile phones

Since the introduction of the Apple iPad in 2010, tablets have quickly become commonplace. The number of children who own one rises each year, with an estimated 55% of three to four year olds using tablet computers in the UK (Ofcom, 2016). In contrast to desktop and laptop computers, touchscreen tablets provide a more intuitive interface that is easier for young children to navigate. Furthermore, tablets are light and can be easily carried by little hands, which means they can be incorporated into play activities and used flexibly in classrooms. The average four year old has no difficulty executing many of the required actions, such as tap, slide and swipe. However, advanced movements such as double tapping and selecting can be more challenging. The key characteristic of the tablet, the use of finger touch on screen, seems to appeal to young children but also meets their learning needs. One study, which compared the use of a tablet with stylus versus tablet with finger and compared again to paper and pencil, found three to five year olds made more progress in learning to write capital letters when using the tablet with finger (Patchan & Puranik, 2016).

While preschoolers will often need help from an adult, four year olds often have frequent access to smartphones. UK surveys indicate that, once set up, young children happily play games or browse through photos and videos on their mum or dad's phone (Plowman et al., 2012).

### *Learning from touch screen apps*

Young children, over the age of two, can learn effectively using apps on touch screen devices. Art applications, for example, allow interesting marks to be made very easily. This immediate feedback encourages interest in preschoolers and keeps young children engaged longer, often more so than with traditional paint and paper (Price, Jewitt, & Crescenzi, 2015).

Numeracy and literacy development can also be supported through touch tablets. For example, four year olds can practise estimating number values, arranging numerical values in order of magnitude, and recognising Arabic numerals. Mark making can be encouraged through drawing apps, where children can create letter like symbols or use pre-existing letters to create made up words or their friends' names.

---

**Parent post – video chatting with little kids**

*My family lives far away, so we use Skype to keep in touch. My two year old frequently talks to my mum and other relatives using the video link. She seems to understand that her grandmother on the video is the same one that visits twice a year. However, I wonder how much she really understands, both about the people on the video and the conversations that they have. Also, is using the screen at her young age negatively impacting on her development?*

---

If you've ever interacted with a baby, you've probably noticed how much she has enjoyed playing back and forth games. You blow a raspberry, she laughs, you tickle, she giggles, and so on and so on. It's not just babies, all young children are very sensitive to whether or not you are responding to them. It's as though they know that an adult who is responsive is likely to be a good person to keep close by and learn from. This is important in regard to digital relationships. Young children are able to form a relationship and learn over video chat, as long as their video partner is responsive (Myers et al., 2016). Video calling is a good way for children to keep up relationships with loved ones who are far away. The screen time, if kept to a reasonable limit, should not be a cause for concern.

## Frequently asked questions – screen time

### Can children learn from non-interactive video content?

In general, research suggests that young children learn less well from the screen than they do from real life. For example, in learning a new task, two year olds will need to see video instructions multiple times, but they will learn the task after only one live demonstration (Anderson & Pempek, 2005).

In regards to language learning, children two years and older can clearly learn new words from screen content. However, there is once again a video deficit and children learn better from a live person.

### Can children learn a second language through television or radio?

In infancy, children are able to distinguish all phonetic contrasts. That means that they can tell apart the small sounds relevant in understanding any spoken language. Over time, this range narrows to focus on those relevant to the languages which surround them, whether inside or outside of the home. Some studies have investigated whether children who hear a foreign language through the radio or video will retain the relevant phonetic contrasts. In fact, research shows that a live speaker is required for sensitivity to the heard language to be retained (Kuhl, Tsao, & Liu, 2003).

### Why is there so much violence in children's cartoons?

Violence is a traditional component of many cartoons, with violent actions occurring even more frequently than in an adult live action drama. Often violence is presented in a silly way, where no one ever gets hurt. Some researchers think that this is unhealthy for children and leads to desensitisation or trivialisation of violence. In fact, research demonstrates that children are less likely to behave in an aggressive manner after seeing violence which has been presented in a funny way (such as in *Scooby Doo*), compared to more realistic depictions (Kirsh, 2006).

Violence has always been thought to be appealing to children. However, some research contradicts this, showing that children get more enjoyment from content that does not contain violent acts (Weaver et al., 2011). Additionally, many options are now available which do not contain violence and instead present a slow paced and more realistic representation of reality.

**Is it ok to leave the TV running in the background?**

Not much is known regarding the potential impact of adult background television on the development of young children. We do know that time spent in imaginary play and socialisation with adults is very valuable for a child's development. Therefore, if the TV is interrupting play or taking your attention away from your child, you may wish to turn the TV off or set up play for your child in a quiet area.

**Are children more likely to develop attention disorders if they spend a lot of time looking at screens?**

While a very common parental concern, this is one of those questions where the answer is difficult to disentangle. Correlational studies show that children with attention difficulties watch more TV. But it's not clear which way the causal relationship goes. Children who have difficulty maintaining attention are drawn to the fast paced nature of child led programming. Also, parents often find TV a very effective way of calming active children down, so they are more likely to encourage it. Unfortunately, without randomly assigning groups of children to a TV watching schedule, we can't say whether or not TV is influencing difficulties with attention. In the absence of hard data, moderation would appear to be the most sensible approach.

## Resources

American Academy of Pediatrics. (2016). Policy statement: Media and young minds. *Pediatrics*, *138*(5). http://doi.org/10.1542/peds.2016-2591

American Academy of Pediatrics, Committee on Public Education. (2001). Children, adolescents, and television. *Pediatrics*, *107*(2), 423–426. http://doi.org/10.1097/00000542-196803000-00034

Anderson, D. R., & Pempek, T. A. (2005). Television and very young children. *American Behavioral Scientist*, *48*(5), 505–522. http://doi.org/10.1177/0002764204271506

Bellissimo, N., Pencharz, P. B., Thomas, S. G., & Anderson, G. H. (2007). Effect of television viewing at mealtime on food intake after a glucose preload in boys. *Pediatric Research, 61*(6), 745–749.

Bus, A. G., Takacs, Z. K., & Kegel, C. A. T. (2015). Affordances and limitations of electronic storybooks for young children's emergent literacy. *Developmental Review, 35,* 79–97. http://doi.org/10.1016/j.dr.2014.12.004

Cheung, C. H. M., Bedford, R., Urabain, I. R. S. De, Karmiloff-Smith, A., & Smith, T. J. (2017). Daily touchscreen use in infants and toddlers is associated with reduced sleep and delayed sleep onset. *Nature Publishing Group,* April, 1–7. http://doi.org/10.1038/srep46104

Christakis, A. D. A., & Michelle, M. (2013). Modifying media content for preschool children: A randomized controlled trial. *Pediatrics, 131*(3), 431–438. http://doi. org/10.1542/peds.2012-1493

Christakis, D. A., Gilkerson, J., Richards, J., Zimmerman, F., Garrison, M., Xu, D., Gray, S., & Yapanel, U. (2009). Audible television and decreased adult words, infant vocalizations, and conversational turns. *Archives of Pediatric and Adolescent Medicine, 163*(6), 554–558.

Garrison, A. M. M., Liekweg, K., & Christakis, D. (2011). Media use and child sleep: The impact of content, timing, and environment. *Pediatrics, 128,* 29–35. http://doi.org/10.1542/peds.2010-3304

Kirsh, S. J. (2006). Cartoon violence and aggression in youth. *Aggression and Violent Behavior, 11,* 547–557. http://doi.org/10.1016/j.avb.2005.10.002

Kuhl, P. K., Tsao, F., & Liu, H. (2003). Foreign-language experience in infancy: Effects of short-term exposure and social interaction on phonetic learning. *PNAS, 100*(15), 9096–9101.

Moser, A., Zimmermann, L., Dickerson, K., Grenell, A., Barr, R., & Gerhardstein, P. (2015). They can interact, but can they learn? Toddlers' transfer learning from touchscreens and television. *Journal of Experimental Child Psychology, 137,* 137–155. http://doi.org/10.1016/j.jecp.2015.04.002

Mumme, D. L., & Fernald, A. (2003). The infant as onlooker: Learning from emotional reactions observed in a television scenario. *Child Development, 74*(1), 221–237.

Myers, L. J., Lewitt, R. B., Gallo, R. E., & Maselli, N. M. (2016). Baby FaceTime: Can toddlers learn from online video chat? *Developmental Science,* 1–15. http:// doi.org/10.1111/desc.12430

Ofcom. (2014, 2016). *Children and Parents: Media Use and Attitudes Report.* Available at www.ofcom.org.uk

Patchan, M. M., & Puranik, C. S. (2016). Using tablet computers to teach preschool children to write letters: Exploring the impact of extrinsic and intrinsic feed-back. *Computers & Education, 102,* 128–137. http://doi.org/10.1016/j.compedu. 2016.07.007

Plowman, L., Stevenson, O., Stephen, C., & McPake, J. (2012). Preschool children's learning with technology at home. *Computers & Education, 59*(1), 30–37. http:// doi.org/10.1016/j.compedu.2011.11.014

Price, S., Jewitt, C., & Crescenzi, L. (2015). The role of iPads in pre-school children's mark making development. *Computers & Education, 87,* 131–141.

Robb, M. B., Richert, R. A., & Wartella, E. A. (2009). Just a talking book? Word learning from watching baby videos. *British Journal of Developmental Psychology, 27*, 27–45. http://doi.org/10.1348/026151008X320156

Weaver, A. J., Jensen, J. D., Martins, N., Hurley, R. J., Wilson, B. J., & Jensen, J. D. (2011). Liking violence and action: An examination of gender differences in children's processing of animated content. *Media Psychology, 14*, 49–70. http://doi.org/10.1080/15213269.2010.547829

Zimmerman, F. J., Christakis, D. A., & Meltzoff, A. N. (2007). Television and DVD/video viewing in children younger than 2 years. *Archives of Pediatric and Adolescent Medicine, 161*(May), 473–479.

Becky Cameron

# 5 My preschooler has no interest in letters or sounds

## Should I be worried?

**Parent post – dyslexia**

*My four year old refuses to learn her letters. She doesn't recognise any of the alphabet, and won't write anything approaching a letter. She will let me read her storybooks, but doesn't show any interest in following along. When I point out letters and words that we see around town, she runs away and does something silly. At preschool they can't get her to participate in any of the phonics activities. We do have dyslexia in the family and I'm wondering if I should have her assessed. What should I do?*

Books can be great fun. Reading for preschoolers means spending time in the world of bunnies on scooters and ballerina dogs. Pair this with one on one time with loved ones, and what could be better? Well, not a lot! It is hard to oversell the benefits of books and shared reading. Not only does reading together support a child's language development, it can also create a feeling of closeness and prepare our child for a good night's sleep.

### Does my preschooler have dyslexia?

Reading is not a source of joy for all children or, for that matter, parents. Most preschoolers will pick up short words and letter sounds easily, but a small group will struggle. This may be worrying for parents who see other children the same age starting to read. While struggles with the alphabet can be a sign of literacy difficulties, parents should not be overly concerned. Nursery is a time for getting to grips with written language and how it works. However, this can also be done later. At preschool age, children should feel relaxed about their learning and be led by their interests. If parents have ongoing concerns, these should be mentioned to the teacher at the start of school, where special support can be given.

### *What is involved in learning to read?*

For children to be able to read, they have to do two things. Firstly, they need to take the words off the page. So they have to decode, or transform, written symbols into meaningful language sounds. This is what phonics is for. But reading also requires linguistic understanding. Your child needs to understand the meaning of what she has read. This is where knowledge of words, vocabulary, sentence structure and grammar are important.

Children with reading difficulties most often struggle at the first hurdle, decoding. While most reading research tells us that phonics is an effective method for teaching children to learn to read (US National Reading Panel, 2000). It is also clear that it doesn't work for all children (Justice & Ezell, 2004).

### *What is dyslexia and why does it occur?*

A child with what has traditionally been known as dyslexia will not be skilled in getting the words off the page. However, her vocabulary will most likely be good, as will her linguistic understanding. A child with dyslexia will really struggle with any task that requires representing, holding and/or using individual speech sounds. Some children experience reading problems related to their vision or their motivation to learn, or they have a developmental difficulty which impacts on all of their learning. While these children have reading problems requiring additional support, they would not be considered to have dyslexia.

The primary causes of dyslexia are not well understood. We do know that it is related to how the brain develops, and that there is a strong genetic component. We also know that dyslexia runs in families (Barry, Yasin, & Bishop, 2007). According to one theory, children with reading problems may show differences in how they process the rhythmic information in speech (Kuppen & Goswami, 2016). This would explain the difficulties children with dyslexia have in breaking a word down into its constituent sounds. It would also explain their difficulties in matching individual speech sounds to letters and letter combinations, as required in synthetic phonics programmes.

Struggling with learning to read is no fun for children or parents. The good news is that children who are at risk for reading difficulties are now identified and supported early on. In the UK, a national phonics screening takes place in the summer of Year 1, at the approximate age of six. In this test, children are asked to read a list of nonsense and real words. This measures the extent to which a child has learned her letter to sound correspondences. Children who fail are given the test again the following year. All schools will put support measures quickly in place for those children not reaching the published government benchmark.

In the US ongoing monitoring of various types is used to pick up struggling readers and to tailor ongoing support programmes. The No Child Left Behind act monitors the yearly progress of schools in accordance with state based assessments. To receive this source of federal funding, a constant improvement in standards must be evidenced. This means that schools will have a strong incentive to bring all children up to a competent level of reading.

## The science of learning to read

The development of early literacy is strongly tied to our understanding and knowledge of spoken language. For example, whether or not a child can break down the spoken word *dog* into three separate sounds (d-o-g) is a really good predictor of how easily she will learn to read. This is because most English speaking children will be taught to match sounds (phonemes) to letter symbols (graphemes) in early reading instruction. The more we talk and read with our children, the more experience they will have of spoken language and how language sounds combine to make words. All this exposure makes gaining early literacy skills easier.

### *What is phonics all about?*

Before any formal teaching, first reading usually comes through recognising a word as a picture. For example, your child may recognise and say aloud 'McDonald's', when she sees the sign. As she is recognising the word as a whole, without understanding how the letters map onto sounds, this isn't full reading. However, using a visual strategy like this can work for a while. Things get tricky when words that look similar sound different and mean different things. So, for example, it's hard to remember how *top* and *tap* differ, and which one is pronounced which way, if you don't know how the individual written and spoken sounds match up. This knowledge is also essential for learning to spell words correctly.

The teaching of phonics begins early in most English speaking countries. In the UK, all children begin a programme of synthetic phonics by the age of five. In most cases this happens even earlier, when children are aged four. Systematic phonics instruction is used in early literacy training in most English speaking countries. Some US classrooms use a whole word recognition approach. This is where a child learns the meaning and sounds of words as a whole, rather than dividing them up into smaller units. Children are taught to recognise words in relation to other words, and in the larger context of what they are reading.

Synthetic phonics teaches the matching of phonemes, which are the smallest meaningful sounds in language, to their written correspondences, graphemes. So, for example, the letter *s* corresponds to a *ss* sound (as in *snake*). While *s* has an obvious pronunciation, some letters do not. For example, the pronunciation for *e* may be not be intuitive for some parents. In synthetic phonics, spellings are introduced alongside the developing phonics knowledge.

Parents who would like to help with phonics learning may find it useful to look online where there are spoken examples for each letter. Many schools ask parents not to teach letter names, but rather letter sounds, as this can cause confusion. The advantage of knowing some of the basic letter sounds is that your child can blend them together to form a simple regular word like *sat*.

Research shows that early awareness of the sounds that make up words is a good predictor for ease in learning to read. So, for example, preschool children who are able to answer the question 'what is brake without the *b* sound?' will learn to read without much trouble. In fact, this task is quite tricky for many five year olds. It is thought that syllables are fairly easy for young children to pick out. Around half of preschool children are able to identify the syllables within a word (Liberman et al., 1974). However, awareness of smaller divisions in words, such as phonemes, comes slightly later at around school age (Gross & Treiman, 1996).

### *How can I support my child in learning to read?*

Sharing books is just one of the many ways to support reading readiness. Developing knowledge of spoken language, particularly learning to hear the individual sounds in words, can be very helpful. Familiarity with language sounds will help your child to feel more comfortable when entering school and starting formal literacy learning. One way of achieving this is through song. Early years' songs and nursery rhymes often emphasise and exaggerate the sounds in language. There are a huge number of free resources available online and in public libraries. Enjoying these together can be both fun and helpful for your child.

## Nursery rhymes and reading development

Nursery rhymes are a great way to support early literacy. For example, in one project, young children who recited rhymes each day saw a benefit in early literacy skills (Kuppen & Bourke, 2017). Rhyming couplets can draw a child's attention to how the sounds within words can be both similar and different. For example, think of this verse in a popular nursery song: *twinkle twinkle little star, how I wonder what you are.* *Star* and *are* rhyme, but *star* combines an *s* and *t* sound at the beginning of the word before the rhyme. Also, although they sound the same, they are spelled differently, which introduces the complexity of written to spoken correspondences, a real issue in a language like English.

Not only are rhymes great for supporting early literacy, they are also very popular with children. This is why we come across them so frequently in children's picture books and songs. Using rhyming words creates a natural rhythm and a sense of anticipation. It also makes the verse more memorable. Many poems or nursery rhymes use a strong metre or rhythmic pulse; just think of the *twinkle twinkle* example above. Nursery songs can encourage this rhythm and repetition by using a strong beat and musical accompaniment. The melody can also help a child to remember the words.

Maybe you remember this rhyme, which has been popular with preschoolers for decades: *Two little monkeys jumping on the **bed**, one fell off and bumped his **head**, momma called the doctor and the doctor **said**, no more monkeys jumping on the **bed**!* It is a great example, as the rhythm in the language makes toddlers want to jump on a bed. The use of action in conjunction with rhymes also makes the verse more memorable. The particular genius in this nursery favourite is that it involves naughty behaviour and some finger wagging at the end.

### Parent post – boys and reading

*I have two boys, one is ten, and the other is four, and just about to enter school. My husband and I are voracious readers and spend a good deal of our spare time reading novels and non-fiction. We have recently been disappointed to see our eldest son refuse to read. He has decided that 'reading is for girls' and he wants to spend his free time playing football or watching TV, and nothing else! I blame his friends, who are very anti-school. I really want to avoid this happening with our youngest. I wonder how best to convince him that reading is cool and something fun to do?*

## Getting boys into reading

While we all know great boy readers, study after study shows that as a group boys underperform in reading. A recent evaluation of the Programme of International Student Assessment (PISA, a survey of more than half a million 15 year olds) showed a global trend of boys lagging behind in their reading (from 2000 and 2010; Stoet & Geary, 2013). In general, boys appear to prefer non-fiction. They are also more likely to choose books which do not challenge them, and may skip sections and read less accurately than girls. While teachers may help to address these issues, there is a larger problem. Boys are not reading for pleasure. Reports suggest that girls, not boys, read for fun. Girls also read more often. This becomes increasingly true as children enter the teenage years. As a general pattern, boys become more negative in their attitudes towards reading as they move into secondary school (Logan & Johnston, 2009).

Many parents ask what they can do to encourage a culture of reading coolness. In many cases, this is down to individual schools or communities. However, there are also a few things that parents can do.

1   Take your child to a library/bookshop and let him choose one book and you choose another.
2   Give books as presents. Choose something that you think will appeal to your child's interests. Or encourage relatives/friends who have a good relationship with your child to select a book, when they want to give a gift.
3   You do the reading. With younger children this is a given. But with older children it can be very appealing to be read to, particularly when you read with expression, doing the voices, etc.
4   Love reading yourself. Spending your free time curled up with a book sends a strong message to your children.
5   Play a game with your reading. Each time you get to a word your child recognises, let him read it out. Or if he is a reader, have him do one of the voices, reading every time the quotation marks come up.

### ACTIVITIES TO SUPPORT EARLY LITERACY IN PRESCHOOLERS

**Share picture books.** Picture books with large print and small amounts of text are best. The pictures should illustrate exactly what is happening in the story.

**Point with your finger to the words as you read them.** This can help children associate the spoken with the written word and might not be something we do intuitively. Research shows this can help early reading development (Justice & Ezell, 2004).

**Discuss the plot of the story.** What is happening and why? Are any choices being made? What would happen if another action was taken? How could things have turned out differently?

**Ask about the feelings of the main character.** Why is he angry? How do you feel when you are angry? What makes you angry?

**Point out written words when you are out.** Words that have already caught your child's eye will be the most effective. But also your child's name on her coat hook, or signs telling us what to do, or where to go, will work too. Anything that might be of particular interest will draw her attention to the written letters.

**Learn some nursery rhymes together.** Recite them while jumping on the bed (if that's allowed in your house – if not, then bang with sticks). The rhythm together with the spoken rhymes will help to underline the segments in the words.

**Put your child's name on everything.** The more you practise writing it out, the more she will recognise the letters and sounds and understand that letters and words represent spoken language.

**Make a journal together.** This can be anything – a few pieces of paper stapled together. Or let her choose how she wants to make it. Encourage your children to write a few words (squiggles) and draw a picture about what happened today.

**Use magnetic boards and letters.** This will increase familiarity and your child will most likely remember some of the letter sounds (s, a, t, p, i, n are good ones to start with).

**Practise tracing first letters.** This can be fun to do in the sand, in sugar, with finger paints, shaving foam, whatever you have to hand. Capital letters are usually easier to start with.

**Provide lots of opportunities for drawing.** The fine motor skills used for drawing are the same as those that will be used when holding a pencil and forming first letters.

**Play I-spy.** Say to your child 'I spy something that begins with shhh . . .' and then let her guess the object (shoe) that you've spotted nearby. This helps to highlight awareness of speech sounds in words.

**Learn tongue twisters together.** Such as: *she sells seashells by the seashore.*

**Play clapping games.** Such as: Miss Mary Mack, where you create a rhythm through repeated clapping actions and rhymes.

**Use alphabet books.** Ideally ones with fun memorable pictures for each of the letters.

TIPS ON HOW TO BOOK SHARE WITH PRESCHOOLERS

There are certain things we can do to make the most of sharing a book. The following suggestions will provide many opportunities for supporting language and literacy development. When asking questions, it is best to make them into a conversation to avoid your child feeling like she is being tested.

1   Go to the library and allow your child to choose a book. Ask her, 'Why did you choose this book?'
2   Take a look at the front cover. Ask, 'What do you think this book is about?'
3   Begin reading the book in a way where you can both see the text and images. Follow along the text with your finger. Ask a series of other open ended questions. For example, 'What is happening in this picture?'
4   Use any opportunity to name colours, quantities, emotions and actions and to describe objects.
5   Respond and listen attentively, smiling and nodding a lot. Extend from what your child has said. 'Oh yes, she's at the shop, what do you think she's going to buy?'
6   Occasionally, choose a book which has just pictures and no text. Encourage your child to make up the story from the pictures.

## Frequently asked questions – reading

### What is the best routine for reading at night?

The best routine is one that works for the family. Many parents allow a child to choose a book after bath time. They then look through it and read it together; after that it's lights out and sleeping. Some parents may allow more than one book or may choose the book themselves. Other parents may prefer a book with no pictures at night time as this might encourage the child to switch off and relax into sleep.

### My little girl always wants to read the same story. Is this ok, or should I be insisting on reading a variety of books on lots of different topics?

Research shows that children benefit from re-readings of their favourite story. After multiple readings, children are more likely to learn the book vocabulary, and also gain further understanding of the story (Trivette et al., 2012). So, don't worry if your child always grabs for the same book. When the time is right, she will follow your lead to pick up something new from the bookshelf.

**What is the typical age for a child to start reading?**

In the UK, children are introduced to phonics at age four and start this in earnest at age five. Most children are reading simple words at age five/ six and, from this point onwards, progress at their own rates. Some children will have been taught to read at home and will be able to read at age three. However, most parents will wait for formal instruction from school. In the US, children are taught to read in school at age six.

**Given differences in reading attainment, are single sex primary schools good for children?**

Evidence supporting the different competencies in girls and boys is often put forward as demonstrating the appropriateness of single sex education. Unfortunately, it is difficult to compare performance in the two types of schools as there are so many factors which differentiate school type outside of whether or not they are single or mixed sex. Because of these complications, it is unclear whether or not single sex primary schools benefit our children. However, one study using random assignment of children to secondary schools in Korea found children in single sex schools achieved higher college entrance exam scores (Park, Behrman, & Choi, 2013). Unfortunately, even this study is confounded, as the single sex schools were private, and the mixed sex schools were publicly run.

## Resources

Barry, J. G., Yasin, I., & Bishop, D. V. M. (2007). Heritable risk factors associated with language impairments. *Genes, Brain, and Behavior*, 6(1), 66–76. http://doi.org/10.1111/j.1601-183X.2006.00232.x

Gross, J., & Treiman, R. (1996). Children's sensitivity to syllables, onsets, rimes, and phonemes. *Journal of Experimental Child Psychology*, 61, 193–215.

Justice, L. M., & Ezell, H. K. (2004). Print referencing: An emergent literacy enhancement strategy and its clinical applications. *Language, Speech, and Hearing Services in Schools*, 35(2), 185–93.

Kuppen, S. E. A., & Bourke, E. (2017). Rhythmic rhymes for boosting phonological awareness in socially disadvantaged children. *Mind, Brain, and Education*, 11(4), 181–189.

Kuppen, S. E. A., & Goswami, U. (2016). Developmental trajectories for children with dyslexia and low IQ poor readers. *Developmental Psychology*, *52*(5), 717–734.

Liberman, I. Y., Shankweiler, D., Fischer, F. W., & Carter, B. (1974). Explicit syllable and phoneme segmentation in the young child. *Journal of Experimental Child Psychology*, *18*(2), 201–212. http://doi.org/10.1016/0022-0965(74)90101-5

Logan, S., & Johnston, R. (2009). Gender differences in reading ability and attitudes: Examining where these differences lie. *Journal of Research in Reading*, *32*(2), 199–214. http://doi.org/10.1111/j.1467-9817.2008.01389.x

National Reading Panel. (2000). National Instititute of Child Health and Human Development, Washington, DC. Available at www.nichd.nih.gov

Park, H., Behrman, J. R., & Choi, J. (2013). Causal effects of single-sex schools on college entrance exams and college attendance: Random assignment in Seoul high schools. *Demography*, *50*(2), 447–469. http://doi.org/10.1007/s13524-012-0157-1

Stoet, G., & Geary, D. C. (2013). Sex differences in mathematics and reading achievement are inversely related: Within- and across-nation assessment of 10 years of PISA data. *PLoS ONE*, *8*(3). http://doi.org/10.1371/journal.pone.0057988

Trivette, C. M., Simkus, A., Dunst, C. J., & Hamby, D. W. (2012). Repeated book reading and preschoolers' early literacy development. *Center for Early Literacy Learning*, *5*(5), 1–13.

Becky Cameron

# 6   My two year old isn't talking!

**Parent post – two year old not talking**

*My son is two years old and has only ever said 'mama' and 'no'. Even with those, I'm not sure that they were proper words, and not just accidents! He is a happy, energetic little boy, who mostly does as I ask. He can go up the stairs while holding on to the handrail, and kick a ball with no problem. I told myself I wouldn't worry, but now that his second birthday has come and gone, I am starting to get concerned that he's not talking. We've had a try, but he won't even copy animal sounds or wave bye-bye. What should we do?*

Most children learn to talk quickly and easily. However, it is not unusual to see two year olds who don't talk much. Estimates from the US suggest around 14 per cent of 18 to 24 month olds are not talkers (Horwitz et al., 2003). While many of these children are 'late bloomers' and will go on to catch up with their peers by school age, a small group will have prolonged speech and language difficulties. Children who are late to talk may be more likely to worry, or feel angry, and may need extra help to communicate their feelings (Desmarais et al., 2008). Getting access to the right support is important.

## How to spot a language problem in a two year old

If you are a parent of a late talker, the first step is to talk to your doctor. In your discussions, she will want to rule out the possibility of hearing issues. This is because hearing difficulties can be related to slow speech development. Your doctor will also ask questions about how much language your child understands. It is best to try to assess this as objectively as you can. If your child hears well but appears to understand little of what you say, she is at risk for language problems (Thal, Tobias, & Morrison, 1991). Risk for speech and language impairments can sometimes be picked up in infancy, when clinicians observe abnormal cries or social responses. However, more often, problems are spotted when parents interact with other children and realise their own child is not hitting the developmental milestones. For this reason, a parent's role in observing her child's language is really important.

### What causes speech and language difficulties?

When a child is unable to produce speech correctly or fluently, she has a speech disorder. However, when there are difficulties understanding spoken language or expressing thoughts or ideas, then it is a language disorder. Developmental language disorder (DLD) is most often recognised through a difficulty in expressing meaning in words and sentences, in the absence of another intellectual or developmental condition. However, children with this impairment may also have difficulties understanding meaning in language. Estimates suggest that around 7 per cent of children have DLD (see www.asha.org). Amongst this group, a seven or eight year old might speak at the level of a typical three year old. She will say things such as 'Anna goed there' instead of 'I went there'. She might also have difficulties understanding meaning, confusing who did what in the sentence – 'The boy chased the cat'. The causes of developmental language disorder are not well understood. However, twin studies show clearly that genetic make-up is a strong indicator of which children will develop language impairments (Bishop, 2006).

It may be difficult to know what to do if your two year old is not talking. If you're seeing a number of the following behaviours, you may wish to talk to her doctor:

- Your child is saying very few, or no, words.
- When you give a direct instruction, e.g. 'Go get me a nappy', she does not appear to understand.
- When your child plays, she does not engage in imaginary or symbolic play (where an object stands for something else – e.g. a banana is used as a telephone).
- She is consistently demonstrating challenging behaviour which you find difficult to manage.
- She uses few gestures such as pointing etc. (clinical risk indicators taken from Prelock, Hutchins, & Glascoe, 2008).

---

**Parent post – learning to talk**

*I am just so amazed by my little girl. She has just turned one and is starting to say her first words. She says 'jus' when she wants juice and 'mama' when she sees me. I have never taught her any words, and I find it fascinating that she has started talking all by herself. How does this work? Are there stages of talking that all children pass through?*

---

A child's first word is a landmark achievement. It's all happened over such a short time, and she still seems so little! Pointing and calling out even the most basic *mama* or *ball* or *doggy* is the result of an incredible amount of learning. To start with, there's an association which has been made between words and objects or concepts. Then, there's the spoken language she has had to process to get to this point. To try to understand what it must be like, imagine that you have gone to a country where you don't understand the language. When someone speaks to you, it sounds like one long combination of sounds. As the pauses and rhythm of the language don't mean anything to you, you've got no idea where one word begins or ends. Your infant faces a similar dilemma. Very early on, she will need to learn to identify single words, for example *ball*, in the continuous stream of speech. She will then need to pair up the sounds of the spoken word *ball* to the correct object. There's also the tricky matter of getting the tongue and lips arranged correctly to produce the necessary word sounds. This is not to mention the thinking processes needed for her to put her thoughts into words.

When considered altogether, it's not surprising that many parents are awed by the magic of their child's first words. It all happens in a very short space of time. Infants achieve this by having a flexible brain, which prioritises input from the world of speech and social interaction. Our children are particularly interested in us as parents or carers. So in the early years it's hugely important to spend lots of time talking and giving loads of one to one specialised attention. Our children are listening to us, even, it would appear, before they are born.

## The stages of language development

### Infancy

Our first steps in learning to talk begin in the womb. The foetus receives sounds which are filtered through the noises of circulation and digestion.

However, the mother's voice can still be heard, and the characteristic changes in stress and pitch remain. Over time, the foetus becomes familiarised to the characteristic patterns of the native language. She will also recognise the trademark rhythm of her mother's voice. In fact, when mothers repeatedly read the same book aloud in the third trimester, infants recognise and prefer these stories after birth (DeCasper & Spence, 1986). This suggests infants are learning about language even in the womb.

Perhaps this explains how, soon after arriving to the world, infants can already distinguish subtle differences in language sounds. For example, they can show us that they hear a *ba* sound as different from a *pa* sound (Eimas et al., 1971). They also have particular preferences for learning about language. So, for example, when three month olds are looking at pictures of talking heads, they prefer images where the mouth movements match the vowel sounds they are hearing, rather than showing a mismatch (Kuhl & Meltzoff, 1982). This may be because matched examples provide better opportunities for learning.

### *Infant directed speech and joint attention – supporting infant language development*

Have you heard that cooing talk that parents use for their babies? You may think of it as baby talk. Much as it may aggravate some adults, babies love it and benefit from it. When your child hears this distinctive speech, she perks up and pays attention, knowing that what you are saying is specifically for her. The term psychologists use is infant directed speech. It is the sing-songy way mums, dads, brother, sisters, grandfathers, grandmothers and people across the world speak to young children. Infant directed speech is typically slower, overall higher pitched, but with more variation than in adult directed speech. It usually has longer pauses, uses repetition and has a simple sentence structure.

While you may have thought it annoying, speaking to young children in this way is actually developmentally appropriate. It may encourage a child's language development. For example, placing key words at the end of a sentence such as 'Look, there is the *dog*', and stressing the final word, may actually help vocabulary learning. The use of exaggerated pauses, emphasis, as well as ups and downs in pitch, may also help your child to more easily identify where one word begins and ends.

Infant directed speech is not the only way in which we can support early language development. A very simple behaviour known as joint attention is another example. Joint attention is when both you and your child look at something together, or look at each other. Although a small action and something you may often do without thinking, it can be really effective. Imagine you are both looking at a dog and you say, 'Look at that lovely big brown dog over there'. In this case pointing may also be helpful. With these instructions, it is likely that your child will be able to pick out the dog from the scene. Over time, she will learn to associate what she sees with not only the word *dog* but also the adjectives *lovely*, *big* and *brown*. Noticing and making sure that you and your child have joint attention when talking together is something you can easily add to your everyday activities.

## Saying her first words

Most children will pass through pretty standard stages in their journey to talking. In the first months, many of the noises you will hear coming from your baby are the result of body processes. However, one exception is cooing, which is the repetition of vowel-like sounds and occurs anywhere between one and four months. Soon after this point, babbling begins and canonical babbling, where consonant–vowel strings are pronounced, e.g. *babababa* or *dadadada*, appears at around seven months (average ages from data provided by Kuhl & Meltzoff, 1996). First words, which have typically appeared by the first year mark, are often combined with nonsense babbling sounds. Babbling in these later stages varies greatly from child to child. However, some sounds are easier to pronounce, and *b* and *p* sounds are very popular, so will likely be heard a fair bit.

In the early stages, a child's vocal tract more closely resembles that of a monkey than an adult human. This is because it is not designed for talking but for getting milk from the breast as efficiently as possible. Very young children have a tongue that is larger, and a vocal tract that is smaller, than an adult human's. This limits what type of vocal sounds can be made, and means that a child's speech is easy to identify. However, there are also other limitations. Our children need to have the experience of listening to speech. Evidence from deaf infants shows that these children are delayed in their language development and sound slightly different in their babbling (Oller & Eilers, 1988). This is likely because deaf children can't hear themselves, or others, when they are experimenting with speech sounds.

### *What will my child's first words be?*

Young children are keen to tell others what they want. For example, *more juice* is one pretty common two word combination in early language development. Also, most young children are interested in communicating to create social bonds. They want to join in with social games and affectionate interactions which keep loved ones close.

In this context, the words your child will learn first are those which are most interesting and useful to her. First words are most often nouns, such as people, animals and objects. This is because the things that exist in our environment are easy to label, much easier, for example, than identifying abstract concepts, such as 'I am hungry'. Studies commonly show that Daddy, Mummy, Bye, Hi, Uh-oh, Bottle, Dog, Ball, Baby, Duck, Cat, Banana, No (Tardif et al., 2008) appear very early in development across languages.

New words are initially added to your child's repertoire at a fairly slow rate. While there is a huge range in what is typical, one British study put two year olds as understanding around 80 words and speaking around 60 (Hamilton, Plukett, & Schafer, 2000). Your child's ability to understand words will proceed much more quickly than her ability to say them, although sometimes the words she understands are not always the same words that she says! While this may be surprising, the ease of language comprehension versus production is not. Just think of a foreign language that you do not know very well. Now think how much easier it is to understand what someone else is saying to you, compared to trying to answer them using the appropriate vocabulary, accent and grammatical structure.

Traditionally, it was suggested that children undergo a vocabulary spurt towards the end of the second year, and reach a rate of 10–20 new words per day. New research shows that the spurt is only the case for a minority of children and most children make steady gains over their development (Ganger & Brent, 2004).

## Combining words

After gaining a small spoken vocabulary, maybe 50 words or so, children begin to put words together. Although it may seem like a small thing, in fact putting words together can really increase your child's power of expression.

Often two word combinations can start off quite simply. For example, *Mummy shoe.* In this instance, without context, we don't know whether the child is indicating that the shoe belongs to Mummy, or whether she wants Mummy to take or give the shoe. Assuming the former, she can easily extend the word combination to *Daddy shoe* and *Daddy coat.* With experience, your child will become more sophisticated at combining words and will become aware of the importance of word order and context. However, you will hear some items such as *police car* or *fruit pot* that are not actually two word combinations. Here, the child has learned the two words as one and so they lose flexibility as individual items.

### *How can I help my child to make two word combinations?*

If you would like to encourage word combinations, and your child already has a small spoken vocabulary, you can try to model some two word examples. You could try making this into a teasing game, where your child can use her own name (if they can say it!), which might make it more fun. So you could say 'Mummy's teddy' and if they respond with a shake of the head and say 'No! Fred teddy', great; or if they just say 'No', you can model a desired response for them or make it into a question, 'Mummy's teddy?'

## Language development at two and three

Over the ages of two and three, your child will make great leaps in the length and complexity of her spoken language. Again, there is a wide range in terms of what is normal. Some children will be producing telegraphic speech, which consists mostly of noun and verb combinations. Others will be saying full sentences of 20 words or more. Beyond the age of three, language is well established and your child will demonstrate the basics of grammar, which will continue to develop into the school years.

Around the ages of two and three, you may notice a gradual change in the social and communicative nature of your relationship. Talking together means that you can both express your wants and needs. It may also be possible to come to agreeable solutions through reasoning, negotiation or striking a bargain.

Children of this age are managing some big feelings, and the development of speech can allow these to be communicated. The sharing of frustration, anger and sadness can increase your feelings of closeness. Not only is talking fundamental in the development of family relationships, it is also important for establishing relationships in the outside world. This is particularly key if your child is participating in play groups, group child minding, or is in a nursery setting. The communication of wants and needs allows your child to relax in the knowledge that she will be catered for, and may lower any feelings of anxiety she may have. It can also minimise the need to resort to physical outbursts.

#### TIPS FOR GETTING HER TALKING

**Talk to your children.** Children whose parents talk to them a lot have larger vocabularies (Huttenlocher et al., 1991). If you're not sure what to talk about, narrate what you're doing or what you can see and ask simple questions that you think your child might be able to answer.

**Use child directed speech.** This means using short and simple sentence structure and vocabulary. It can also be helpful for children to have you slow down your speech and make exaggerated but natural pauses. This helps children to pick out individual words from the stream of speech. Placing stress on the key words and/or putting them at the end of a sentence is also helpful – 'Look at the *doggy*. The *doggy* is going for a *walk*.'

**Get your child's attention.** Young children rely on bodily cues and joint attention when learning new language. It is very helpful if you can gain the attention of your child and direct it to the subject while talking, for example, 'Look, a cat'.

**Take your lead from what your child is saying.** For example, if she says 'digger', you can respond, 'Yes, there is a digger working on the street'. In this example you are both confirming and extending. Confirming you have understood what she has said by saying 'yes' (this is a good feeling for your child) and extending the topic to provide more information and further opportunities for vocabulary and grammatical learning. In younger children picking up on the focus of your child's attention is particularly helpful for learning new words. Children between one and two years of age learned words better if the objects were already the focus of attention when labelled (Tomasello & Farrar, 1986).

**Extend the conversation.** You can do this by asking a question, e.g. 'What do you think the digger is doing?' or 'What colour is the digger?' depending on the words your child may be likely to know.

**Adjust your use of language according to the abilities of your child**. For children who are just beginning to string two or three words together, it may be helpful to use a large proportion of commands, requests or yes/no questions (Barnes et al., 2008).

**Use familiar routines to create language developing opportunities.** Children need context to develop their language. Familiar routines such as bedtime allow for children to pair up *time to lie down and go to sleep* with the actions of going to bed. Routines also allow children to understand more abstract concepts, such as associating the feeling of being hungry with the time for lunch, etc.

**Read picture books together frequently.** Picture books provide frequent opportunities for learning new language, particularly object names. Storytime also sets the scene for a quiet time for talking through stories and gaining increased interest from your child in what you are saying.

# Frequently asked questions – learning to talk

### Should I buy toddler targeted DVDs? Will they help language development?

The research is mixed on whether video media can support language development in early childhood. While some information can be retained, it is generally agreed that children learn better from us (Krcmar, Grela, & Lin, 2007). This may be because we give our children immediate, responsive feedback (Lauricella et al., 2010). Research supporting this conclusion demonstrates that children can learn new verbs over Skype, where a responsive adult is present, but not through watching traditional one-way video (Roseberry, Hirsh-Pasek, & Golinkoff, 2014). See the chapter on screen time for further discussion on this topic.

### Why do babies babble?

There are two main alternative explanations for why babies babble. One suggests that babies babble to gain practice for talking, while the other suggests they are simply practising moving their mouth. In recent experiments, the first argument has gained support, suggesting that babies are indeed trying out language sounds in preparation for first words (Holowka & Petitto, 2002).

### Will teaching baby sign mean my child will learn to talk faster?

Baby signing classes are a popular activity for parents and infants, and take place across countries and languages. They are appropriate for infants aged between eight and thirteen months. After this, a child will likely be talking and will no longer need to sign.

In baby sign, children are offered a simplified means of communication using hand actions to represent everyday words. Advocates of baby sign suggest children learn to produce signs on average one month before they produce their first word (Goodwyn & Acredolo, 1993). However, a review of the evidence finds no significant difference in the age at which children produce signs as compared to words. There has also been no evidence to suggest baby sign speeds up the rate at which a child learns to talk (Johnston, 2005).

### Will my child be slower to talk because he is a boy?

It is not uncommon for boys to be less interested than girls in language supporting activities, such as close interaction with parents or joint attention (Whitehouse et al., 2012). However, evidence which demonstrates a slower average rate of vocabulary development in boys (Bauer, Goldfield, & Reznick, 2002) also shows that the sexes eventually average out (Wallentin, 2009). Boys are at a higher risk for more serious incidences of language delay and disorder (Zubrick et al., 2007).

### Will my second child be slower to talk than my first?

First words and when a child starts to talk vary hugely, with most children falling into the typical range by around school age. In general, first born children tend to get a lot more child directed speech, compared to subsequent siblings. Research suggests this has advantages and disadvantages. While second born children are often slower to learn their first fifty words (Pine, 1995), they also hear language being used in context. Most helpful is the simplified speech directed towards their older sibling. This may be why second, or subsequent, children often use the pronouns *you* and *me* earlier. They have a much larger experience in overhearing the use of pronouns, which change in relation to who is doing the talking.

### Why do parents refer to themselves as Mummy or Daddy? Is this helpful for children?

As discussed above, learning personal pronouns, such as *you* and *me*, can be difficult for children as they switch depending upon the speaker. For example, a parent refers to her daughter as *you* and herself as *me*, but of course this reverses when the child is speaking. Referring to oneself in a consistent manner, e.g. Mummy, can provide clarity for young children. However, most children will have mastered the basic personal pronouns by the time they are three. Referring to oneself as Mummy/Daddy is no longer necessary after this point.

### Can using dummies/pacifiers affect speech development?

Some clinicians have suggested that using a dummy or pacifier may reduce babbling, an activity which is supportive of language development. While this has been a concern for some parents and nurseries, studies addressing this question have shown no significant differences in language development (Shotts, McDaniel, & Neeley, 2008). In regard to long term pacifier use, most doctors will suggest that dummies are no longer as useful after six months. They should, in most situations, no longer be used after the age of two, as this is related to greater risk of inner ear infection (Rovers et al., 2008).

**My son is two years old and not talking. Someone suggested I go to see a clinician. What would an appointment with a speech therapist look like?**

A first appointment with a speech and language therapist (SLT) will involve you giving a history of your child's development and expressing your concerns in relation to your child's language. Often the therapist will play alongside your child and engage her in an attempt to assess her level of communicative ability. Once an assessment has been made, an appropriate level of support will be suggested, and a personal programme will be developed for your child.

## Resources

American Speech–Language–Hearing Association. (n.d.). Page on Spoken Language Disorders (incidence and prevalence). Available at www.asha.org

Barnes, S., Gutfreund, M., Satterly, D., & Wells, G. (2008). Characteristics of adult speech which predict children's language development. *Journal of Child Language*, *10*(1), 65–84. http://doi.org/10.1017/S0305000900005146

Bauer, D. J., Goldfield, B. A., & Reznick, J. S. (2002). Alternative approaches to analyzing individual differences in the rate of early vocabulary development. *Applied Psycholinguistics*, *23*(3), 313–335. http://doi.org/10.1017/S014271640 2003016

Bishop, D. V. M. (2006). What causes specific language impairment in children? *Current Directions in Psychological Science : A Journal of the American Psychological Society*, *15*(5), 217–221. http://doi.org/10.1111/j.1467-8721.2006. 00439.x

DeCasper, J., & Spence, M. (1986). Prenatal maternal speech influences newborns' perception of speech sounds. *Infant Behavior and Development*, *9*, 133–150.

Desmarais, C., Sylvestre, A., Meyer, F., Bairati, I., & Rouleau, N. (2008). Systematic review of the literature on characteristics of late-talking toddlers. *International*

*Journal of Language & Communication Disorders / Royal College of Speech & Language Therapists, 43*(4), 361–89. http://doi.org/10.1080/13682820701546854

Eimas, P., Siqueland, E., Jusczyk, P., & Vigorito, J. (1971). Speech perception in infants. *Science, 171*(3968), 303–306.

Ganger, J., & Brent, M. R. (2004). Reexamining the vocabulary spurt. *Developmental Psychology, 40*(4), 621–32. http://doi.org/10.1037/0012-1649.40.4.621

Goodwyn, S. W., & Acredolo, L. P. (1993). Symbolic gesture versus words: Is there a modality advantage for onset of symbol use? *Child Development, 64*, 688–701.

Hamilton, A., Plukett, K., & Schafer, G. (2000). Infant vocabulary development assessed with a British communicative development inventory. *Journal of Child Language, 27*, 689–705. http://doi.org/10.1017/S0305000900004414

Holowka, S., & Petitto, L. A. (2002). Left hemisphere cerebral specialization for babies while babbling. *Science, 297*(August), 1515.

Horwitz, S., Irwin, J., Briggs-Gowam, M., Bosson Hennan, J., Mendoza, J., & Carter, A. (2003). Language delay in a community cohort of young children. *Journal of the American Academy of Child & Adolescent Psychiatry, 42*(8), 932–940. http://doi.org/10.1097/01.CHI.0000046889.27264.5E

Huttenlocher, J., Haight, W., Bryk, A., Seltzer, M., & Lyons, T. (1991). Early vocabulary growth: Relation to language input and gender. *Developmental Psychology, 27*(2), 236–248.

Johnston, J. C. (2005). Teaching gestural signs to infants to advance child development: A review of the evidence. *First Language, 25*(2), 235–251. http://doi.org/10.1177/0142723705050340

Krcmar, M., Grela, B., & Lin, K. (2007). Can toddlers learn vocabulary from television? An experimental approach. *Media Psychology, 10*, 41–63.

Kuhl, P., & Meltzoff, A. (1982). The bimodal perception of speech in infancy. *Science, 218*, 1138–1141.

Kuhl, P., & Meltzoff, A. (1996). Infant vocalizations in response to speech: Vocal imitation and developmental change. *Journal of Acoustical Society of America, 100*, 2425–2438.

Lauricella, A. R., Pempek, T. A., Barr, R., & Calvert, S. L. (2010). Contingent computer interactions for young children's object retrieval success. *Journal of Applied Developmental Psychology, 31*(5), 362–369. http://doi.org/10.1016/j.appdev.2010.06.002

Oller, D. K., & Eilers, R. (1988). The role of audition in infant babbling. *Child Development, 59*, 441–449.

Pine, J. M. (1995). Variation in vocabulary development as a function of birth order. *Child Development, 66*(1), 272–281.

Prelock, P. A., Hutchins, T., & Glascoe, F. P. (2008). Speech-language impairment: How to identify the most common and least diagnosed disability of childhood. *Medscape Journal of Medicine, 10*(6), 136.

Roseberry, S., Hirsh-Pasek, K., & Golinkoff, R. M. (2014). Skype me! Socially contingent interactions help toddlers learn language. *Child Development, 85*(3), 956–970. http://doi.org/10.1111/cdev.12166

Rovers, M. M., Numans, M. E., Langenbach, E., Grobbee, D. E., Verheij, T. J. M., & Schilder, A. G. M. (2008). Is pacifier use a risk factor for acute otitis media? A dynamic cohort study. *Family Practice*, *25*(4), 233–236. http://doi.org/10.1093/fampra/cmn030

Shotts, L., McDaniel, D., & Neeley, R. (2008). The impact of prolonged pacifier use on speech articulation: a preliminary investigation. *CICSD*, *35*, 72–76. Available at www.asha.org/uploadedFiles/asha/publications/cicsd/2008STheImpactofProlongedPacifierUse.pdf

Tardif, T., Fletcher, P., Liang, W., Zhang, Z., Kaciroti, N., & Marchman, V. A. (2008). Baby's first 10 words. *Developmental Psychology*, *44*(4), 929–38. http://doi.org/10.1037/0012-1649.44.4.929

Thal, D., Tobias, S., & Morrison, D. (1991). Language and gesture in late talkers: A 1-year follow-up. *Journal of Speech, Language and Hearing Research*, *34*, 604–612. http://doi.org/10.1044/jshr.3403.604

Tomasello, M., & Farrar, M. J. (1986). Joint attention and early language. *Child Development*, *57*(6), 1454–63. Available at www.ncbi.nlm.nih.gov/pubmed/3802971

Wallentin, M. (2009). Putative sex differences in verbal abilities and language cortex: a critical review. *Brain and Language*, *108*(3), 175–83. http://doi.org/10.1016/j.bandl.2008.07.001

Whitehouse, A. J. O., Mattes, E., Maybery, M. T., Sawyer, M. G., Jacoby, P., Keelan, J. A., & Hickey, M. (2012). Sex-specific associations between umbilical cord blood testosterone levels and language delay in early childhood. *Journal of Child Psychology and Psychiatry, and Allied Disciplines*, *53*(7), 726–34. http://doi.org/10.1111/j.1469-7610.2011.02523.x

Zubrick, S. R., Taylor, C. L., Rice, M. L., & Slegers, D. W. (2007). Late language emergence at 24 months: an epidemiological study of prevalence, predictors, and covariates. *Journal of Speech, Language, and Hearing Research : JSLHR*, *50*(6), 1562–92. http://doi.org/10.1044/1092-4388(2007/106)

Becky Cameron

# 7 Why has he started lying?

### Parent post – why is he lying?

*My son will be four next month, and he has recently started lying. What I find really upsetting is not the lie itself, but that he swears to me he's telling the truth. When presented with the indisputable facts, I ask him why he's telling me things that aren't true. I explain how it makes me feel, but he says he doesn't mind. He says he wants to be naughty. He says he doesn't like me, and that he feels happy when I am sad. I know he's only testing, but it still hurts! He has always been so kind and considerate. We have such a loving relationship. I don't know what's changed. Is this just a phase?*

It's not nice to see your child lie. It can feel pretty uncomfortable, particularly if she's trying to get someone else in trouble. While it's easy to feel disappointed, in reality all children lie at some point. When children are very little, their lies are more like fanciful stories, something like 'Mum, I just saw a dinosaur riding the bus!' Full blown anti-social lies don't really occur until the age of three. At four, children know that lying is morally 'wrong', but that won't necessarily stop them from doing it!

## Why do children lie?

There are two types of lies. The first are called pro-social or white lies. These are lies that spare the feelings of others, and are considered polite behaviour. For example, saying a present is liked, when it is not. The second type of lie is anti-social, and what we generally associate with lying behaviour. In this situation, the lie works in the favour of the lie teller, and is told at the expense of others. Most parents and teachers are very concerned to stop this type of lying. Perhaps because of this, most children of nursery age are aware that 'lying is wrong'. However, they still do it. It is very common to hear lies such as 'I didn't hit my brother', 'I didn't take her toy', 'I didn't cheat', and so on.

So why do children deliberately lie? Most often, children lie to get out of trouble. However, some children are more prone to lying and lie more frequently, in a larger variety of situations. One experiment addressed why this might be. In this research a group of four year olds were introduced to a toy spider. The children were encouraged to pet it, but while they did, the experimenter pushed a button to make the spider jump. Most children were surprised and slightly scared. The size of each child's startle reaction was measured. Analyses showed that the children who were not particularly startled by the jump were the same children who lied most frequently (Zwirs et al., 2014). This suggests that physiological factors may be related to whether or not our children lie. Lying successfully also requires quite a few advanced thinking skills. As a result there is a developmental progression in how well children lie.

## Lying in young children

At age two, children say things that they know aren't entirely true. However, this isn't full blown lying. To be able to deceive, your child needs to hold a lot of relevant information in her head. She needs to think through the implications of the lie, and how it relates to the information she should provide. Aditionally, in order to lie successfully, she must have a good understanding of how minds work. For example, she must grasp that seeing leads to knowing. Or in other words, she must understand that when we have seen her take a chocolate from the box, there is no point in lying about it. With well developed thinking skills, your child is much better able to create convincing lies which stand up to interrogation.

Many four year olds are accomplished liars, but even they may reveal the truth when questioned. Preschoolers will often uncover their lies by not carrying through the logical implications of what they have said. For example, in a research experiment, a group of two and three year olds were asked to not peek at a toy. Some 80 per cent of the children did not follow this instruction and peeked when the experimenter wasn't looking. When asked if they had looked, most two year olds admitted that they had, but many of the older children lied. However, when asked follow up questions, the three year olds that had lied forgot to conceal that they knew the identity of the toy (Evans & Lee, 2013). In this way, they exposed that they had peeked.

## Do children understand 'white lies'?

White lies are trivial lies, or lies done out of politeness. Knowing when to tell a lie to spare someone's feelings is a complicated issue. Despite this, politeness lies or social flattery can be seen in four year old children, likely due to heavy coaching by adults. In one experiment, while three year olds rated a drawing the same no matter who was in the room, four year olds were kinder if the illustrator was present. Four year olds also rated drawings higher for individuals who were known to them (Fu & Lee, 2007). Experiments such as this highlight four years of age as the point for the emergence of social lying behaviour.

## Lying and moral development

Moral development relates to our understanding and behaviour in relation to issues of justice, fairness and human rights. As children, we have a pretty black and white understanding of good and bad. However, even young children can see shades of grey, depending upon the situation. For example, a three year old can see that not sharing a toy has different moral implications compared to, for example, not putting a toy back in the correct place (Smetana, 1981).

As children we build our view of right and wrong based on those around us. It's not just what parents and other authority figures say, it is also what they do. So, to be good role models, we should not be dishonest with others. We should be having explicit discussions on what is expected in a trusting relationship, such as open and honest communication.

A deep understanding of moral issues and behaviour requires a good deal of maturity. This is beyond the reach of most preschoolers. However, supporting the development of a child's moral conscience lays the foundation for further moral development.

## The developing conscience

Toddlers are increasingly aware of social rules. They are also very happy to point out when others have broken these rules. At the age of three, most children grasp the basics of responsibility. However, their behaviour varies widely when faced with moral choices.

Moral decisions in childhood are often guided by the conscience. Conscience in this case means the feelings of discomfort when doing something known to be against the approval of those in charge. As your child's conscience is developing, so are her self-awareness, self-control and understanding of the behaviour of others. From the second year onwards, you will start to see more pro-social behaviour in your child, as she takes more care in the choices she makes.

Related to pro-social behaviour is your child's level of sympathy or empathy for others. In many cases, even young children will act in an attempt to help those who are distressed. They will often show concern when others are frightened or worried. This may be related to a child's previous experiences. For example, children who have observed unkind behaviour towards an adult are more likely to be pro-social without any need for encouragement (Vaish, Carpenter, & Tomasello, 2009).

### How can we support moral development?

The best way you can support your child's moral development is to use care and sensitivity in your own behaviour. This is in regard to decisions and actions within your family, but also within the wider community. As she learns to express herself, your child will feel more comfortable discussing her feelings with you. This is where closeness is particularly important. For a relationship to feel loving, your child must know that, at some level, you are on her side. She must feel that her thoughts and feelings matter, and must feel liked and valued by you as a person.

Within a close relationship, discussion is very effective. Together, you can explore the connection between her experiences and the feelings they generate. Your sensitive responding during these discussions will guide her to develop moral understanding in a loving context. If, in a calm and close moment, it can be explained why a certain behaviour was unacceptable, the message can become internalised. In this way, a child can think to herself, for example, 'I am not going to take something without asking, because it goes against the wishes and feelings of those around me.' This is an internal motivation. It is preferable to thinking 'I am not going to take something because I will get into trouble for it.' This is an example of external motivation, and thinking of this type does not support mature moral behaviour. Using rational, emotionally balanced language when discussing unwanted behaviour with our children is related to higher levels of conscience formation and moral development.

TIPS TO ENCOURAGE TRUTH TELLING

- Starting to have discussions on the importance of telling the truth from an early age (probably around two) can help.
- Asking a child to promise to tell the truth can promote truth telling in some children. However, this should only be used for the odd, important occasion.

- You can decide to encourage honesty above all else. So if your child has behaved badly and lied about it, the repercussions should be different from those where she has behaved badly but told you the truth.
- Talk over times when you have struggled to tell the truth in difficult circumstances, but how it was the best thing in the end.

## TIPS ON HOW TO ENCOURAGE PRO-SOCIAL BEHAVIOUR

- Make sure your child is listening when discussing unwanted behaviour. If she is not listening, leave her until she is ready to hear you. Discussion the next day can lead to greater internalisation of moral feeling than in the heat of the situation.
- When talking through misbehaviour, focusing on the child's actions and the consequences of her actions for others may help.
- It is recommended to always ask for and listen to your child's opinion. If possible, incorporate their viewpoint into your discussion.
- It can be helpful to talk though the effect of your child's behaviour on another: 'When you scream, it hurts my head.' 'If you take away his toy, it makes him feel sad.'
- Research suggests that discipline that uses a high amount of power to achieve goals (physical punishment or threats), where a child is motivated to behave through fear of punishment, will not help her to develop her own sense of right and wrong. This will mean she is unlikely to act pro-socially when an authority figure is absent.
- Giving responsibilities such as assigning caring or helping duties for a younger sibling can be beneficial.
- When making decisions as a family, attempt to give everyone a say and, if possible, have a vote.
- Some research demonstrates that telling a child that she has a good reputation will decrease her likelihood of future cheating (Fu et al., 2016). Giving children positive labels can help them to build self-esteem and behave pro-socially.
- Reading stories with a moral component can provide an opportunity for good conversations. Children who were read stories where a main character was rewarded for showing good moral behaviour were subsequently more likely to behave in a pro-social way themselves (Lee et al., 2014).

## Frequently asked questions – lying

### How can I tell if my child is lying?

Sadly, there is no lie detector test for children. The best technique is to know your child well and look for unusual behaviours, such as avoiding eye contact, noticing any touching of face, biting of lip, fidgeting or repeating of the question (as in stalling for time to think of an answer). However, these actions may also have a completely innocent explanation! Younger children may also be likely to shout or respond aggressively, or defensively, when telling a lie.

### How can I encourage moral thinking in my child?

Parents who guide independent thinking, and use a questioning style in their conversations, have children with higher levels of moral reasoning.

### How can I tell if my child is developing a strong sense of right and wrong?

If your child feels guilt or remorse after anti-social behaviour, she is likely developing some sort of internal code for moral behaviour.

### Are some children easier to guide towards pro-social behaviour?

Just like adults, children vary in how much their conscience guides their behaviour. Your child has her own personality, which is strongly guided by her temperament. Individual differences in personality will dictate her desire to be pro-social and follow your lead. Children who are responsive, and often imitate a parent's actions (for example, cleaning a table), show greater moral maturity at age three (Forman, Aksan, & Kochanska, 2004).

### What can nurseries do to promote good moral development?

There is a great deal that nurseries can do to guide moral development in the children they care for. For example, group settings are a perfect place for children to learn about sharing. Adults and older children can demonstrate good sharing behaviours, which can be copied by younger observers. Play, which involves a shared goal, can promote goodwill amongst the children, and encourage trust and working together. Preschoolers can also be taught that other children have their own viewpoints. Nursery can be an ideal setting to highlight individual backgrounds, cultures and experiences which may be different from their own.

### Is it ok to lie to my child?

Research has shown that when a young child realises an adult has lied to her, she is more likely to lie herself (Hays & Carver, 2014). If you wish to promote a truthful relationship, lying is best avoided.

### Should I try to make my child feel guilty after she has behaved badly?

Guilt can be felt in relation to empathy with a parent, or the person hurt by the anti-social behaviour. In older children, it can also be felt because a child feels she has let herself down, and not reached the standards she has set for herself.

In order to reach mature moral understanding, it is important to reflect on our own behaviour. Our children should be encouraged to do this, particularly in relation to how our behaviour impacts on others. Guilt can be a strong motivator and, in moderation, can help to promote pro-social behaviour. However, parents should not attempt to make children feel guilty on a regular basis. Saying things which are overly emotional and personal will not support your child's ability to take on the moral message of what you are saying. This approach will also not be effective in promoting pro-social behaviour long term.

### Why are some preschool children concerned with making up and making things better, while others don't appear to be bothered?

It is clear that some children crave resolution and approval more than others. These differences are likely down to the individual temperament of the child, and parenting practices. For example, some research has shown that children with high levels of anxiety, with parents who use low-power disciplining techniques, have high levels of conscience development (Kochanska, 1991) and may be more ready to seek resolution.

### My toddler is very bad at sharing; does this mean that she has poor moral development?

We've all seen toddlers who don't want to share. Grabbing a toy away from another child, with a 'I need it', is very natural behaviour for a young child. It does not mean that she is naughty or has been poorly socialised. Learning the benefits of sharing, being respectful and cooperating with others are part of a child's moral development. Moral understanding develops in tandem with the maturation of our thinking processes. To be able to undertake reasoned action when faced with moral quandaries requires sophisticated thinking and knowledge about the world. Toddler aged children are in the early stages of this process. They are primarily driven by impulses which satisfy their own needs. It is up to us to guide our children to a more self-controlled, pro-social outlook.

### My preschooler cheats every time we play a game. What should I do?

It is very common for preschoolers to cheat at games. In some cases, children may not understand that their behaviour breaks the rules. Others may identify the lack of fair play, but not consider it cheating. No matter how they see it, it is usually the case that children who break the rules to their advantage do so to win.

If the frequent cheating of your preschooler is concerning you, there are a few things that you can do to try to tackle it. The first is to frequently discuss the importance of honesty over winning. The second is to have low-key expectations, or at least make it clear that it doesn't matter who wins. Finally, if you constantly highlight when she cheats, letting her know that she is not going to get away with it unnoticed, she might do it less frequently.

# Resources

Evans, A. D., & Lee, K. (2013). Emergence of lying in very young children. *Developmental Psychology*, *49*(10), 1958–1963. http://doi.org/10.1037/a0031409

Forman, D. R., Aksan, N., & Kochanska, G. (2004). Toddlers' responsive imitation predicts preschool-age conscience. *Psychological Science*, *15*(10), 699–704. http://doi.org/10.1111/j.0956-7976.2004.00743.x

Fu, G., Heyman, G. D., Qian, M., Guo, T., & Lee, K. (2016). Young children with a positive reputation to maintain are less likely to cheat. *Developmental Science*, *19*(2), 275–283. http://doi.org/10.1111/desc.12304

Fu, G., & Lee, K. (2007). Social grooming in the kindergarten: The emergence of flattery behavior. *Developmental Science*, *10*, 255–265. http://doi.org/10.1111/j.1467-7687.2007.00583.x

Hays, C., & Carver, L. J. (2014). Follow the liar: The effects of adult lies on children's honesty. *Developmental Science*, *17*(6), 977–983. http://doi.org/10.1111/desc.12171

Kochanska, G. (1991). Socialization and temperament in the development of guilt and conscience. *Child Development*, *62*(6), 1379–92.

Lee, K., Talwar, V., McCarthy, A., Ross, I., Evans, A., & Arruda, C. (2014). Can classic moral stories promote honesty in children? *Psychological Science*, *25*(8), 1630–1636. http://doi.org/10.1177/0956797614536401

Smetana, J. G. (1981). Preschool children's conceptions of moral and social rules. *Child Development*, *52*, 1333–1336.

Vaish, A., Carpenter, M., & Tomasello, M. (2009). Sympathy through affective perspective taking and its relation to prosocial behavior in toddlers. *Developmental Psychology*, *45*(2), 534–543. http://doi.org/10.1037/a0014322

Zwirs, B. W. C., Szekely, E., Herba, C. M., Verhulst, F. C., Jaddoe, V. W. V., Hofman, A., Ijzendoorn, M. H. van, & Tiemeier, H. (2014). Social and non-social fear in preschoolers and prospective associations with lying about cheating. *International Journal of Behavioral Development*, October. http://doi.org/10.1177/0165025414553136

Becky Cameron

# 8    What can my newborn do?

## Parent post – what can infants do?

*I'm totally confused about what infants are capable of. Some things I've read say tiny infants are mini-scientists and work out many things for themselves. Others say they are completely helpless, and rely on us entirely. Which is it?*

There has long been a misunderstanding about babies. A well known nineteenth century psychologist said babies see the world as one 'great, blooming buzzing confusion' (William James, 1890, *The Principles of Psychology*, p. 462). We now know that this simply is not true. Babies come pre-programmed for learning, and are very choosey in how they focus their attention. Babies tune into the things that matter and quickly block out those that don't. They also come equipped with a wide range of survival skills. Many of these are related to forming social attachments.

## The newborn's preference for faces

Given that they are completely dependent on others for food, shelter and comfort, it's not surprising that babies are intent on forming emotional bonds. They conduct what appear to be mini love affairs with their primary caregivers. A baby's every behaviour is designed to keep a caring adult close by; their survival instincts are in full effect.

From very early on, experiments show us that babies have brains wired to prioritise social interaction. For example, infants only a few hours old prefer to look at features which resemble a face. While these newborns will pay close attention to a moving head shape, with two eyes, a nose and a mouth, the same two dimensional cut-out with scrambled features is not of much interest (Johnson, Dziurawiec, Ellis, & Morton, 1991).

Clearly, newborns recognise and prefer the human arrangement of facial features. They are also sensitive to where someone is looking, and strongly prefer to look at a face which is looking back at them. Sharing eye gaze supports development, as it promotes effective communication between adult and baby (Farroni, Csibra, Simion, & Johnson, 2002). It also supports attachment.

---

### Parent post – attachment

*What is secure attachment? How do I know if my baby is securely attached?*

---

## What is attachment and attachment behaviour?

Attachment is a term used in psychology to refer to the *connectedness* between individuals. In relation to parenting, it can be understood as the emotional bond that encourages nurturing between you and your child. A secure, or good quality, attachment is what we are all after. In a secure attachment an infant's needs are responded to quickly and sensitively. John Bowlby is the famous figure in attachment theory. He suggests that all humans identify an attachment figure. This is someone near to us who is better equipped to cope with the demands of the world around us. Acting as a secure base, our attachment figure is sought out when we feel stressed or under threat. This physical proximity promotes feelings of protection and security, until we regain our confidence and can return to exploring the world (Bowlby, 1988).

Your newborn is a pro at promoting attachment and eliciting attachment behaviours. In the first days, the infant's primary attachment behaviour is crying. Crying is a very effective tool. It is the most reliable way that newborns can receive attention and care. Infants will cry from pain, for example following an inoculation, as well as from hunger. You will likely hear a hungry cry from your infant if it has been more than three, or three and a half, hours since her last feed. Babies will cry from the cold, which will warm them up, and will cry when put down or left on their own. Some babies will continue to cry even after having been picked up, or may cry for no discernible reason whatsoever! Six weeks marks the peak frequency for crying, and it will decline from this point onwards. By the age of about two and a half months, most infants should be crying in relation to some discernible factor, rather than at apparently random times (Zeifman, 2001).

Smiling is a much less aversive attachment behaviour. As a newborn, most smiles will take place during sleep. However, when she is a bit older, probably around the age of two months, your child will most often be smiling when awake. Early on, familiar faces and voices will be the most common reason to smile. But from about three months onwards she will smile more readily when engrossed in one of her favourite games, peekaboo being a good example (Fogel et al., 2000).

---

### Parent post – why won't she copy me?

*If my friend sticks out her tongue, her baby will copy her. She says that all babies do this. My two month old won't do it at all. Does this mean she's got some sort of delay?*

---

The life of a psychologist is not all work and no play. One well known set of experiments involved sticking a tongue out at a newborn baby! Children just a few hours old have been shown to copy an adult who sticks out his tongue, opens his mouth wide, and makes what looks like a kissing face (Meltzoff & Moore, 1977). While it is fun to try this at home (finally, a science-based excuse for making faces at your baby!), don't feel worried if you don't get a reaction. Many babies will not oblige. In fact it has been questioned whether these babies are imitating at all. Many infants will start a rooting reflex when excited, which can look very similar to tongue protrusion. This is a much simpler explanation. There is also a second question as to how much a newborn can actually see. The poor spatial resolution and contrast sensitivity of the newborn would limit her ability to process facial expressions (Barbu-Roth et al., 2009).

---

### Parent post – what can newborns see?

*I ride the underground every day, and see adults cooing at newborn babies from across the aisle. While the adults seem happy, I'm convinced the baby can't see them. Surely, they are too far away? How much can an infant see over the first few months?*

---

## Newborn sensory abilities and development

### *What can a newborn see?*

A newborn's vision is very immature. She cannot see any detail at a distance. However, she does detect some visual information, primarily related to changes in brightness and the movement of objects. For example, her hands will move in the general direction of an object that you have dangled in front of her face (Von Hofsten, 1982). Also, an infant's stepping reflex can be used as a measure of what she sees. The stepping reflex occurs when a newborn is held upright, with the soles of her feet touching a hard surface. In this position, most infants will move their legs, as if they were walking. When infants are placed upon a projected image of a forward moving checkerboard, they make more steps than when they are placed on a moving pattern of clockwise rotating pinwheels (Barbu-Roth et al., 2009). This suggests that newborns use visual information to guide their actions.

Visual acuity refers to the ability to see the shape and detail of things. An infant's acuity is measured by presenting two images, one alternating black and white stripes, the other a solid screen. To gain a measure of acuity, stripe width gradually gets narrower, until a child can no longer tell the two images apart. Your newborn's acuity is about 40 times worse than an adult's. By six months of age, this has reduced to eight times. Adult levels are reached between ages four and six (Lewis & Maurer, 2005).

Despite poor visual acuity, it is remarkable that newborns only four weeks old can recognise and prefer their mother's face (Bushneil, Sai, & Mullin, 1989). Below you can see a simulation of what a newborn infant might see of faces at different distances (Von Hofsten et al., 2014). Despite poor early vision, infants may be able to recognise their mothers by facial features alone (Bushneil, Sai, & Mullin, 1989), particularly at close distances.

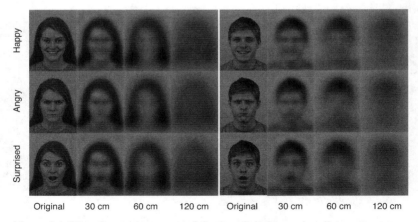

*Figure 8.1* What the newborn sees of the face from increasing distances (reproduced with permission from Von Hofsten et al., 2014).

## Parent post – failed hearing check

*I'm a bit worried about my baby's hearing. We've just come home from the hospital. While we were there, she had a routine hearing check, which she failed. They said not to worry, but does this mean that she is likely to have hearing problems?*

Newborn hearing screening is used to identify children with permanent hearing loss as early as possible. Usually, the test consists of placing a small device in your baby's ear and playing clicks. When you hear sounds, the cochlea, or the inner ear, responds. Screening equipment, which will indicate whether or not your baby has passed the test, picks up this response. If your baby does not pass the screen, it does not necessarily mean that she has permanent hearing loss. She may have been unsettled during the test, or there may have been background noise in the room, or she may have had fluid in her ears. Your baby will be offered another test to confirm her results.

### How well can newborns hear?

After birth, a baby's middle ear and nervous system develop quickly, allowing high pitched sounds to be heard. The processing of lower pitched sounds comes later and reaches adult levels by age ten. A newborn can recognise and show a preference for the sound of a mother's voice (DeCasper & Fifer, 1980). In order to develop mature hearing, children need experience with common sounds. This familiarity will allow them to pick out sounds in the environment (Werner & Marean, 1996).

One sound to which your newborn is particularly sensitive is the crying of other infants. Infants only a few days old will cry to a recording of other infants crying. However, they won't respond to the cry of older infants, or other species, in the same way (Martin & Clark III, 1982). Interestingly, they will also not cry, and will in fact stop crying, if they hear a recording of their own cry.

### What about smelling?

Newborns are amazing in their ability to smell and to root out a mother's nipple. Babies only a few days old can recognise and prefer the smell of their own mother's milk compared to others. This is true even if the infant has had no experience of breastfeeding. The smell also provides comfort. For example, infants undergoing a painful procedure show lowered stress levels (as measured by salivary cortisol) when the air is sprayed with a mist of their mother's breast milk (Nishitani et al., 2009).

TIPS ON GAMES TO SUPPORT ATTACHMENT WITH YOUNG INFANTS

A secure attachment requires parents to be sensitive to their children's needs. So, as a first step, it is important to find a time when your baby would like to play. This will most likely be when she is fed and well rested, and looking around with an attentive, interested face. If she is spitting up, looking away from you or crying, then she needs a break.

Here are some fun things to try:

- peek a boo
- cooing or talking back and forth
- gentle tickling
- dancing
- shaking a rattle
- walk and drop – where you hold your baby in your arms, take two steps and then drop down (bending one knee), and then come back up again, making a rhythmic silly walk.

## Frequently asked questions – babies

### What is attachment parenting and should I be doing it?

Attachment parenting is associated with a number of practices such as breastfeeding on demand, baby carrying, co-sleeping and empathic responding. It is argued by its supporters that these practices promote secure attachments that are in turn thought to relate to positive child outcomes. What parenting strategy you adopt is an entirely personal choice. Read widely and choose an approach that resonates with you, or just follow your instincts.

### Is carrying my baby in a sling a good idea?

Carrying your baby close to you promotes quick and easy responding. It also leaves your hands free to get things done, while still having your infant near to you. In an experimental study, children of mothers given cloth slings to use were more often securely attached than those given plastic infant seats placed near to the mum (Anisfeld, Casper, & Nozyee, 1990).

Carrying skin to skin, known as kangaroo care, is related to improved developmental outcomes in preterm infants (Feldman, Rosenthal, &

Eidelman, 2014). Again this close contact supports sensitive responding but also allows your baby to benefit from your warmth and heartbeat and can help premature babies to regulate their responding.

## Does attachment quality have long lasting effects?

John Bowlby's theory of evolutionary attachment suggests that by age two our attachment experiences contribute to our view of ourselves and others. This is a concept known as the *internal working model*. This model is used to predict and inform our behaviours throughout life. Specifically, it may feed into our expectations when forming future relationships.

The ability to establish an emotional attachment is a highly adaptive feature as it so strongly promotes our survival as individuals. As a result of natural selection, infants are born with a number of attachment promoting characteristics. Babies are tuned into faces and the mother's voice, but additionally humans grasp, root for the breast and spend a good deal of time crying right from birth.

## Do premature babies require special care?

Preterm babies often start life with an extended stay in hospital. This can be stressful for parents and can often get in the way of those first bonding moments with baby. Hospitals, however, are now particularly concerned with providing opportunities for skin to skin contact for baby and caregiver. In many cases, bonding through physical closeness may be a possibility.

Premature children may require ongoing special care. This is really dependent upon the particular circumstances and health of your child. In general, the best advice is to keep a close eye on your child's development. In this way, if any difficulties do arise, you will be able to quickly access the appropriate help.

## Have you heard of the magic baby hold? Does it work to stop babies from crying?

A paediatrician has posted a video of a technique he uses to settle crying babies in his practice. The clip is extremely popular, and the method has become known as the 'magic baby hold'. While it is an appropriate and likely reasonably effective method, it won't work all of the time. For example, it is less likely to work on colicky babies and babies who have been fussing a long time, or in situations where parents are exhausted. The technique involves the doctor folding the baby's arms across her chest with one hand. He then props up the baby's chin with his fingers and, holding her upright and slightly leaning forward, wiggles her back and forth. The method is appropriate for babies up to two to three months old.

### I have heard that it's important to have a parent facing buggy. Is this true?

The evidence supporting the importance of parent facing buggies is very limited. The idea here is that children in a parent facing buggy will be able to see and hear you talking more easily. Parents will also be able to interact with the infant and respond more quickly to the infant's needs. Observational studies have found that conversation with children when out shopping in traditional buggies is limited. However, it's not clear that this would necessarily change with a parent facing setup.

### Why do babies get so upset if you respond to them with a blank expression?

Babies as young as three months know when you're not feeling right, and they don't like it. For example, perhaps you have been interacting, maybe playing a game, and you then stop. If you show no expression on your face, babies will look away frequently, their heart rate will go up, and they will smile less often. If you leave your face this way longer than a couple of minutes, they may even start to cry (Toda & Fogel, 1993). Such experiments have not been run in an attempt to be cruel to young children, but they aim to understand what effects maternal depression may have on our babies. It appears that behaviour such as unpredictable emotional reactions can be stressful for babies and can cause issues related to developing secure attachments.

### Does my baby have any self-control?

Research suggests that infants have innate reactions to experiences designed to bring about an emotional response. For example, a scary face will provoke fear, and blocking access to a toy will provoke anger or frustration. However, how infants react to these provoking situations differs according to temperament. This means they vary in the speed and intensity with which they react to something. There are also differences in a baby's display of self-control, or self-regulation. This refers to how well your baby is able to soothe herself, and whether she uses behaviours such as looking away, sucking or moving close to a caregiver.

**How can I tell whether my baby's smile is for me, or just wind?**

New evidence refutes the conventional wisdom that social smiles, or smiles directed at someone, do not appear until six weeks. Most babies smile in the first month, and parents suggest some of these smiles may be sociable (Addyman & Addyman, 2013). Social smiles are more likely to appear after you've done something silly or unexpected with the desire to amuse your baby. Of course, it's impossible to know for sure. Much to your enjoyment, most infants will be regularly laughing by three months.

**How can we possibly know what infants can do or are thinking?**

It is true that infants have very few means by which to convey thoughts and abilities through behaviour. However, while limited in number, scientists do have a few tried and tested techniques.

In very young children, experimenters rely on tapping inbuilt biological behaviours such as sucking and head turning. In both situations the child will undergo what is called operant conditioning. Here, the infant learns to draw a relationship between performing a certain action, such as sucking quickly on a pacifier or turning the head, and the start of something happening, for example a sound recording turning on. Once the relationship between the two has been learned, an infant can essentially let her wishes be known to the experimenter and conclusions can be drawn.

Another way for an experimenter to explore an infant's thoughts is through what is called habituation. This technique relies on babies becoming bored because they have repeatedly been shown the same thing. The experimenter can then look to see what re-interests her, in this way providing an indication of what has been judged as new by the infant.

A final technique commonly used in infant research is preferential looking. Here, infants are presented with two items and are seated in a way such that only one item can be viewed at a time. The experimenter then records the child's looking behaviour and assesses whether she looks at one item longer than the other. If there is a significant difference between the two, it might be that, firstly, she judges the items as different and, secondly, that she finds one more interesting than the other. The experimenter can then use this information in relation to the questions she is asking.

### I've heard that babies can do maths; what's that all about?

There has been a controversial claim that babies have a general sense of number. So, for example, two spoons are very different from two nappies, outside of their 'twoness'. The question is, can babies see the common ground represented by number? A few studies have suggested that babies as young as six months can tell apart groups where the number of dots differs (in this case, 8 versus 16), even when lots of clues, such as how big the display is, are not available (Xu & Spelke, 2000). This research would suggest that babies have an approximate sense for numbers that develops spontaneously, before experience with counting or any formal arithmetic.

## Resources

Addyman, C., & Addyman, I. (2013). The science of baby laughter. *Comedy Studies*, *4*(2), 143–153. http://doi.org/10.1386/cost.4.2.143

Anisfeld, E., Casper, V., & Nozyee, M. (1990). Does infant carrying promote attachment? An experimental study of the effects of increased physical contact on the development of attachment. *Child Development*, *61*, 1617–1627.

Barbu-Roth, M., Anderson, D. I., Desprès, A., Provasi, J., Cabrol, D., & Campos, J. J. (2009). Neonatal stepping in relation to terrestrial optic flow. *Child Development*, *80*(1), 8–14. http://doi.org/10.1111/j.1467-8624.2008.01241.x

Bowlby, J. (1988). *A Secure Base: Parent–Child Attachment and Healthy Human Development*. London: Routledge. http://doi.org/10.1097/00005053-199001000-00017

Bushneil, I. W. R., Sai, F., & Mullin, J. T. (1989). Neonatal recognition of the mother's face. *British Journal of Developmental Psychology*, *7*(1), 3–15. http://doi.org/10.1111/j.2044-835X.1989.tb00784.x

DeCasper, A. J., & Fifer, W. P. (1980). Of human bonding: Newborns prefer their mothers' voices. *Science (New York)*, *208*(4448), 1174–1176. http://doi.org/10.1126/science.7375928

Farroni, T., Csibra, G., Simion, F., & Johnson, M. H. (2002). Eye contact detection in humans from birth. *Proceedings of the National Academy of Sciences of the United States of America*, *99*(14), 9602–9605. http://doi.org/10.1073/pnas.152159999

Feldman, R., Rosenthal, Z., & Eidelman, A. I. (2014). Maternal-preterm skin-to-skin contact enhances child physiologic organization and cognitive control across the first 10 years of life. *Biological Psychiatry*, *75*(1), 56–64. http://doi.org/10.1016/j.biopsych.2013.08.012

Fogel, A., Nelson-Goens, G. C., Hsu, H.-C., & Shapiro, A. F. (2000). Do different infant smiles reflect different positive emotions? *Social Development*, *9*(4), 497–520. http://doi.org/http://dx.doi.org/10.1111/1467-9507.00140

Johnson, M. H., Dziurawiec, S., Ellis, H., & Morton, J. (1991). Newborns' preferential tracking of face-like stimuli and its subsequent decline. *Cognition*, *40*(1–2), 1–19. http://doi.org/10.1016/0010-0277(91)90045-6

Lewis, T. L., & Maurer, D. (2005). Multiple sensitive periods in human visual development: Evidence from visually deprived children. *Developmental Psychobiology*, *46*(3), 163–183. http://doi.org/10.1002/dev.20055

Martin, G. B., & Clark III, R. D. (1982). Distress crying in neonates: Species and peer specificity. *Developmental Psychology*, *18*(1), 3–9.

Meltzoff, A. N., & Moore, M. K. (1977). Imitation of facial and manual gestures by human neonates. *Science (New York)*, *198*(4312), 75–8. http://doi.org/10.1126/science.198.4312.75

Nishitani, S., Miyamura, T., Tagawa, M., Sumi, M., Takase, R., Doi, H., Moriuchi, H., & Shinohara, K. (2009). The calming effect of a maternal breast milk odor on the human newborn infant. *Neuroscience Research*, *63*, 66–71. http://doi.org/10.1016/j.neures.2008.10.007

Toda, S., & Fogel, A. (1993). Infant response to the still-face situation at 3 and 6 months. *Developmental Psychology*, *29*(3), 532–538.

Von Hofsten, C. (1982). Eye–hand coordination in the newborn. *Developmental Psychology*, *18*(3), 450–461. http://doi.org/10.1037/0012-1649.18.3.450

Von Hofsten, O., Von Hofsten, C., Sulutvedt, U., Laeng, B., Brennen, T., & Magnussen, S. (2014). Simulating newborn face perception. *Journal of Vision*, *14*(13), 1–9. http://doi.org/10.1167/14.13.16.doi

Werner, L. A., & Marean, G. C. (1996). *Human Auditory Development*. Boulder, CO: Westview Press.

Xu, F., & Spelke, E. S. (2000). Large number discrimination in 6-month-old infants. *Cognition*, *74*, B1–B11.

Zeifman, D. M. (2001). An ethological analysis of human infant crying: Answering Tinbergen's four questions. *Developmental Psychobiology*, *39*(4), 265–285.

Becky Cameron

# 9 Is there really a bilingual advantage?

**Parent post – bilingual advantage?**

*I have read that kids who are fluent in more than one language have advantages over monolinguals. Because they are used to switching between languages, or holding back one language while using another, they are better at solving certain types of problems. Is this true?*

More and more parents are making an explicit decision to raise their children as bilinguals. For multilingual families, this is less of a decision and more of a way of life. In the UK, around one third of people can hold a conversation in more than one language. In the US, it's about one quarter. Across the globe, more than half of the world's population uses two or more languages in everyday life. Undoubtedly, learning a second language expands cultural, social and employment opportunities. But is there also a cognitive advantage? Are bilingual children better at certain types of thinking? The answer isn't clear.

## What is the bilingual advantage?

Bilingual children consistently have to monitor a situation, select a language to use, and repress the language(s) not needed. Monolingual children don't do this. Related to these differences, bilingual children may be better at certain tasks. For example, they may be better at controlling their thinking, holding focused attention, or blocking out irrelevant distractions. They may also be better at switching between two sets of rules. For example, they may be better at playing a game where the objective is changed halfway through. The research evidence supporting these ideas is mixed. Some experiments find bilinguals are better at these tasks, while others find no difference between children based on how many languages they speak.

In one popular experiment, arrows are shown on the left or right hand side of a computer screen. Children are asked to press the right arrow key if they see an arrow pointing right, and the left arrow if they see an arrow pointing left. This is the rule, no matter what side the arrow is on. However, most people are faster when the arrows and keys are congruent. In other words, when the right pointing arrow appears on the right side, and the left pointing arrow appears on the left.

The bilingual advantage relates to observations that bilingual children are faster than monolinguals on these and other tasks. In the above example, bilinguals are significantly faster when the arrows and keys are not congruent (Martin-Rhee & Bialystok, 2008). Bilinguals, it is suggested, are more effective at blocking unnecessary information. However, other explanations have also been offered. It may be that differences in performance are down to differences in socio-economic background (Morton & Harper, 2007). Bilingual children, in some studies, may come from homes with a higher family income, and with higher levels of family education. Such criticisms are supported by research which finds no advantage for bilinguals on similar types of tasks (Paap & Greenberg, 2013). These studies may be more effective in controlling for differences between children.

Despite the controversy, there are undoubted benefits to surrounding your child with more than one language. Bilingual children may have a better understanding of things about language, such as the fact that it is mostly random how labels are attached to objects. They may also have a better understanding of how grammar rules work differently in different languages.

Importantly, your child will also have access to a second culture and cultural perspective; she will have the ability to actively communicate in that community and form relationships. A second language may also give her an advantage later in the workplace and offer alternatives in terms of where she can live.

## What does it mean to be bilingual?

Most of us have some knowledge of a second language, but at what point are we considered bilingual? It can be helpful to know how bilingualism is defined. Children who are bilingual are usually from a bilingual family, where one of the parents speaks a different language from that of his/her spouse and from the language spoken in the local environment (known as the majority language). Alternatively, both parents may speak the minority language. In this situation, the majority language is learned in school.

Children can either be actively or passively bilingual. In families where a minority language is spoken, children may understand but not speak the language at home. For these passively bilingual children, home may be the only environment where they come into contact with the non-majority language. Because of this, knowledge of the additional language may not be fully developed. This limited bilingualism can be a real concern for parents who have been determined from the outset to raise a child who speaks two languages. A third option is also available for children who live in bilingual communities or countries. In these situations it is possible for a child to learn an additional language outside of the home, for example where second language schooling is available.

---

### Parent post – communication strategies

*I've heard that if you want your child to be bilingual, you need to have a communication strategy. So, for example, one parent speaks to their daughter only in German, while the other speaks to her only in English. The only problem is that, in our family, my husband doesn't speak German, so we always speak to each other in English. Do you think this will be enough for our daughter to learn to speak both languages fluently?*

---

## How do I raise my child as a bilingual?

### The one person, one language approach

For many families, the choice to raise a bilingual child means that a monolingual home, where a couple speak to each other in a shared language, becomes bilingual with the arrival of their first born child. When there is more than one language between parents, often a clear communication strategy can help. The *one person, one language* approach is a popular two parent family approach, where each parent speaks to the child in a different language. This process begins at birth and a parent makes a conscious effort to speak to his or her child in their chosen language only. This can also be an effective approach when raising a child as trilingual, with two languages spoken at home and one in the community.

The idea behind *one person, one language* is consistency. If each language can be associated with an individual parent, the hope is that young children are less likely to be confused or to mix languages. Whether or not this is an effective method is still up for debate. It is hard to reach a clear conclusion when much of the research is based on small sample sizes, often consisting of researchers' children! However, at least one general conclusion can be made. To have the best chance of raising an actively bilingual child in families where only one parent speaks a minority language, quantity and consistency are key. The minority language should be the only language spoken by the parent concerned, and switching from one language to another should be avoided (Dopke, 1998).

The *one person, one language* approach is just one way in which a child can grow up with more than one language. It is also possible for two parents to speak a minority language, and for the child to learn the majority language at preschool or school. Equally possible is to have a nanny or babysitter who will immerse your child in a second language. The key for giving bilingualism a head start is to have an agreed family plan. It is also important to be enthusiastic, but realistic. Bilingualism is a long journey, which will often require some dedication and hard work.

## Does language develop the same way for monolingual and bilingual children?

While being multilingual used to be considered a disadvantage, we now have a long history of experimental research suggesting the opposite. Since around the 1960s researchers have suggested that, in addition to the advantage of being able to communicate in more than one language, bilinguals have advantages related to how they think.

In terms of language development, bilingual children pass through largely the same milestones at around the same time as monolinguals. However, studies demonstrate that, on average, bilingual children do have smaller vocabularies in each language (Oller, Pearson, & Cobo-Lewis, 2007).

Children raised with more than one language can sometimes be recognised through their habit of mixing up their languages. In some cases, bilingual children are heard using words from one language when speaking in another. This can happen even in conversations with monolinguals who do not understand the speaker's second language. When language mixing happens, it is usually independent of whether or not the parents have adopted a *one person, one language* approach. Most researchers think that children mix languages because some words are associated with a particular language, probably because of the context in which they were learned or the language in which they are most frequently used.

### Parent post 1 – bilingualism blues

*We would like some help on how to raise our daughter as a bilingual. I am French and my husband is American and we live in the US. I have been speaking French to our daughter since birth but she has very little outside contact with the language. Occasionally, she sees her French family for a couple of weeks at Christmas and over the summer break. She watches some TV and short films in French and she listens to some French music, although most of it is in English. She attends daycare full time in English and has done since the age of two. She is now four.*

### Parent post 2 – bilingualism blues

*Recently, our daughter has become a proficient English speaker. However, I've noticed that sometimes when I speak to her in Polish, she does not understand me and is getting frustrated with me speaking my native language. I also find it frustrating that she doesn't understand. She always answers me in English. I would like to know how I can encourage her to speak to me in Polish and try harder to understand me when I speak to her. I used to think, she is little, she will come to speak Polish in her own time, but now I'm not so sure. We are desperate for her to be bilingual and to reap all of the advantages that will offer to her. What can we do?*

As much as parents may want their child to be a bilingual, there is no foolproof way to achieve it. Just as children will vary in their zest for eating vegetables, they will be more or less keen to speak to you in a language that is different from the one they experience outside the home. A few things might raise your chances of success. The first is consistency. If your choice of language is non-negotiable and consistent, children will get the message. Secondly, if you tie the use and experience of the language and culture to things your child enjoys, it is more likely to become associated with positive feelings. This will encourage adoption and use.

TIPS ON HOW TO ENCOURAGE YOUR PRESCHOOL CHILDREN TO LEARN AND ACTIVELY USE A MINORITY LANGUAGE

Provide your child with as much experience in the second language as possible. For example, research demonstrates that the amount of reading to bilingual children in the target language is related to language ability in the target language (Patterson, 2002).

While talking to your child works best, singing or talking along to music, video, TV and radio can be a fun way to keep the minority language heard in the home.

Subscribe to a fun magazine in the minority language; then you can read it together each time it arrives.

Provide incentives for talking in the minority language, such as trips abroad where the minority language is spoken.

Skype with minority language family members so your child can practise what she knows and be proud of her ability.

Cultivate friendships where the children can speak the minority language. Promote it as a special secret language. Your child can meet other children speaking the same language at local weekend language clubs.

You can also use the secret language idea to speak amongst yourselves for rituals such as eating dinner or taking a bath, where the game is that you all must speak the target language.

Encourage responding in the minority language. If your child responds to you in English or the majority language of your community, repeat what she has said in the target language, essentially modelling a desired response.

Try the *one person, one language* approach to see if works for your family.

## Frequently asked questions – raising a multilingual child

### Will my child be smarter because she is bilingual?

There is no evidence suggesting that bilinguals have a higher general IQ. While some experiments show better flexibility of thinking and control of attention, these are isolated abilities, and the evidence to support them is mixed (see main chapter for more details). Put simply, learning two languages is not a route to increasing your child's intelligence.

### Will my child start to talk later because she hears two languages at home?

It is now commonplace for a child to grow up with two languages spoken at home. While there has been some concern that bilingual children will be slower in their linguistic development, there is no conclusive evidence to support this. When considering the two languages together, bilingual preschoolers achieve age appropriate norms

(De Houwer et al., 2013). There is a wide range of ability in what is considered to be typical language development.

### Is my child more likely to learn the language spoken by her mother?

It was once thought that when spoken languages differ, young children are more likely to learn the language of their mother over their father. While this is often the case, the relevant variable is how long the child spends with each parent and how much exposure they have to each language.

### If each parent speaks one language, will our child be bilingual?

It is common to hear advice that in order to not confuse young children, the rule should be one parent, one language. While many parents find this an effective strategy, adopting the *one person, one language* rule does not ensure that children will learn to speak two languages. There are many families in which one parent speaks only a minority language, but the child responds in the majority language. Over time the child may develop a good level of understanding, but is not able to converse in the minority language herself. She is what is known as a passive bilingual. Research shows that if young children respond in the majority language, they are at risk for never fully learning the second language at home (De Houwer, 2007).

Active bilingualism may best be achieved when the minority language is the only one spoken at home. For some families, this requires one parent to speak in her second language. Developing cultural traditions and social networks in the minority language can help to promote positive associations and also support active bilingualism.

### How do we know if our child is getting enough exposure to each language?

The best way to judge if your child is getting good quality interaction with both languages is to monitor her output. If she is speaking predominantly one language, then changes will need to be made in order to achieve active bilingualism. Supporting activities could include attending a Saturday school where the minority language will be spoken.

### Is it worth one parent speaking to the child in a second language only once in a while?

Most experts would consider any second language exposure worthwhile. Although children may only pick up snippets, this may sow the seeds for learning the language later in life.

### What will happen to the minority language when our child starts school?

Children often show a preference for the language spoken at school, which can be at the expense of the minority language. Some children can often refuse to speak anything but the majority language at home, but many parents find they are able to manage through this transition phase. Once the child has passed through the teenage years, it is usually the case that the minority language is fully established.

### Will my child be equally fluent in each language?

Different languages are used for different purposes. It is often the case for bilinguals that the language of education and work is different from the language at home. Therefore, it is unlikely that both languages will be equally fluent at all times across development. Your child's language needs will likely change over time.

### Is there a critical point by which a second language needs to be learned?

If a child is exposed to two languages right from birth, she will readily learn both. While there is no hard and fast cut-off, it is thought that, from around the age of seven, the ease with which a child will pick up a language with no discernible accent tapers off. Additionally, when children move into the teenage years, they may find greater difficulty in gaining full proficiency in a second language. However, there is no critical period as such and children really vary in the ease with which they learn languages. These individual differences can often have a much greater impact than looking to generalisations across age bands.

# Resources

De Houwer, A. (2007). Parental language input patterns and children's bilingual use. *Applied Psycholinguistics, 28*(3), 411–424. http://doi.org/10.1017/S014271640 7070221

De Houwer, A., Bornstein, M. H., & Putnick, D. L. (2013). A bilingual–monolingual comparison of young children's vocabulary size: Evidence from comprehension and production. *Applied Psycholinguistics, 35*(6), 1189–1211.

Dopke, S. (1998). Can the principle of one person–one language be disregarded as unrealistically elitist? *Australian Review of Applied Linguistics, 21*(1), 41–56.

Martin-Rhee, M. M., & Bialystok, E. (2008). The development of two types of inhibitory control in monolingual and bilingual children. *Bilingualism: Language and Cognition, 11*(1), 81–93. http://doi.org/10.1017/S1366728907003227

Morton, J. B., & Harper, S. N. (2007). What did Simon say? Revisiting the bilingual advantage. *Developmental Science, 10*(6), 719–26. http://doi.org/10.1111/j.1467-7687.2007.00623.x

Oller, K., Pearson, B., & Cobo-Lewis, A. B. (2007). Profile effects in early bilingual language and literacy. *Applied Psycholinguistics, 28*(2), 191–230. http://doi.org/10.1017/S0142716407070117.Profile

Paap, K. R., & Greenberg, Z. I. (2013). There is no coherent evidence for a bilingual advantage in executive processing. *Cognitive Psychology, 66*(2), 232–258. http://doi.org/10.1016/j.cogpsych.2012.12.002

Patterson, J. L. (2002). Relationships of expressive vocabulary to frequency of reading and television experience among bilingual toddlers. *Applied Psycholinguistics, 23*(4), 493–508. http://doi.org/10.1017/S0142716402004010

Becky Cameron

# 10 How early is too early for music?

## Parent post – age for music lessons

*I've got a two year old who absolutely loves music! She'll happily dance away to her favourite tunes, while I'm getting on with things around the house. She also loves to have a bash on her xylophone and plastic drums. My husband and I also love music, but neither of us plays an instrument. We have been wondering recently about when might be a good time to start her on some lessons. We have a keyboard in the spare room that we could set up for piano lessons. Does this sound like a good idea?*

Children really enjoy music. Jumping around with an instrument, and singing out to a favourite tune, are great ways to have some fun – particularly if they involve being noisy! As well as providing a good time, music can also help to regulate big feelings. For example, banging on some drums can help get out frustration, while comforting music can help us to calm down or prepare for sleep.

## What is the right age to learn an instrument?

While having access to an instrument is a great idea at any age, more formal instruction is not usually recommended until the age of six at the youngest. There are of course exceptions to this, particularly in highly musical families. In some cases young children will be pestering parents to start earlier, although there are a number of skills required for learning an instrument:

1   Ear training – It is helpful if children can pick out different musical elements such as tone, pitch, rhythm, chords, intervals and melodies through listening.

2   Fingering – Proper finger positioning will be necessary to achieve the appropriate note or note combinations.
3   Motivation – Your child will need either internal (desire to play) or external (rewards based) motivation in order to practise and learn the piano.
4   Concentration – A certain level of sustained concentration will be needed in order to play even a short piece of music.

The appropriate age for starting an instrument can also depend on the system your child's teacher is using. For example, the Suzuki method encourages learning the violin at preschool age, with parent and child attending lessons together. However, most professionals will agree that the following are a good bet for first instruments: xylophone (a child can play with this as soon as she can hold a mallet), drums (same rule applies), piano, violin and recorder (most experts would recommend age six, but younger is also common), guitar (age seven).

## Getting started with music

Young children often have a natural interest in music, even in infancy. You may have seen examples of this, where a baby will stop what she is doing and show intense focused interest, when music begins to play. The ability for music to grab your child's attention continues right into the toddler years. This is often encouraged by toys which make noise or play music. The more annoying the sound effect, the more cherished the toy! But the appeal of musical toys is understandable. A one year old can make a big racket with the simple push of a button. Also, toys which encourage children to push, hit, shake or turn them in exchange for noises or music appeal to the "what will happen if I do this?" inquisitive nature of the toddler. The continuous performance of these little tests allows children to gain a quick understanding of the objects that surround them. It is an important means through which they gain knowledge about the world.

### Early music education

A lot of early years music education, which takes place either in nurseries or in specialist music based groups, is founded on a few well known approaches. The Dalcroze approach, for example, involves something called eurhythmics. This is essentially rhythmic physical movement to music. A typical example would involve children representing musical sounds with movements, such as short sharp actions for drums, flowing movements for triangles and bells, and so on. Kodaly leads children through a singing musical education before any teaching with instruments. For example, simple beats and metres are introduced through listening and singing games, and notation is spoken out in syllables and identified in musical examples. The Orff approach is also popular for children and uses singing, playing and dancing and percussive instruments that can be tapped. Improvisation is encouraged.

## *Singing*

For most children, preschool is too early for formalised music lessons or choirs. However, early years music groups, available through your local library or community centre, are a great idea. Singing tends to be the most easily accessible form of musical experience for most families. It doesn't require an instrument and everyone can join in across all ability levels. When in preschool it's unlikely that your child will be able to hold a tune; she will focus more on the words of the song than the melody. For this reason, singing can sometimes sound more like rhythmic chanting. As awareness of pitch grows, children begin to follow the ups and downs of the melody of the song and most children will be able to sing in tune by age 11 (see table on p. 120). Although it's not necessary to guide your child into accurate singing when young, she will naturally make the most progress if she is able to hear herself when singing and if given appropriate guidance and encouragement. It is important that the songs she learns are at the right level and do not contain lyrics or pitches which are too difficult. If any one element of a song takes too much effort, this will overload your child and singing may become less enjoyable.

A large number of preschooler sing-along CDs are available which will hopefully showcase appropriate singing material. As a general rule, children's songs should not be too high or too low in pitch; they should have short clear phrases, a pace which is not too slow and not too fast, and rhythms that are not too complex.

Although research on preschool singing is sparse, most teachers praise the use of song and its benefits for children. Singing in groups can involve a release of tension, promote feelings of relaxation, increase feelings of happiness, increase attention and concentration, and improve self-esteem (Hallam, 2010). Singing together provides a shared goal and common ground on which to form friendships, and for the very young it offers an opportunity to spend time together in a social setting.

Joint music making offers a great many opportunities for the development of social skills. For example, when preschool children are using instruments in a group setting, they may need to take turns. They may equally need to hold back from playing their instrument until the correct moment arrives. Individual differences in these self-control behaviours, necessary in friendships and successful social interactions, also contribute to what is known as our executive function. This set of skills is related to success in academic areas such as the development of maths and reading abilities (St Clair-Thompson & Gathercole, 2006). Executive function also remains an important predictor of successful career and relationship outcomes (Moffitt et al., 2011). Research further suggests that children who have made music together subsequently act more cooperatively with one another. This is above and beyond children who have been undertaking a similar joint activity (Kirschner & Tomasello, 2010).

### *Rhythmic awareness*

Providing opportunities to learn about rhythm can really benefit your child. As discussed in Chapter 5, being sensitive to the rhythm in speech helps your child to pick out the smaller sounds in language, a key skill when learning to read. Paying attention to the patterns in language, such as which syllables are stressed, also provides infants with cues as to where a word begins and where it ends. This may be why infant directed speech, the sing-songy way in which many adults speak to kids, is so preferred by young children. This type of speech emphasises the rhythmic cues in speech, and may make it easier for children to identify individual words when listening to us talk. Being sensitive to the rhythmic cues in language may also help children to develop more accurate and full knowledge of the individual sounds which make up words. This will make it much easier when a child comes to the task of learning to read and spell. It is very difficult to spell a word if you're unsure how to pronounce it.

**Your child's musical development**

| | |
|---|---|
| 3–6 months | Shows a response to musical sounds |
| | May turn towards the sound and show pleasure or surprise |
| 6 months | Will often sway or bounce to music |
| 2 years | May match movement to music type and rhythm |
| 3 years | Able to learn songs – usually words first, then rhythm followed by melody |
| | Will have difficulty in keeping time for long periods |
| 11 years | Can usually sing in tune although some may find it difficult |
| 11–15 years | Voice change due to physical development, usually between ages of 12 and 14 but can come earlier |

### Parent post – Mozart effect

*I read that if you play Mozart to your unborn baby, she will be more intelligent. This sounds too good to be true. Is it just a myth?*

# The Mozart effect debunked

The suggestion that we can boost the development of our baby in pregnancy attracts a lot of excitement, as well as column inches. The Mozart effect is one such myth, which emanates from research undertaken in the early 1990s. The enduring claim is that playing Mozart to our unborn child will positively affect her intelligence. In fact, the original evidence did not concern babies at all and was related to a short term effect in spatial reasoning seen in university students (Rauscher, Shaw, & Ky, 1993). The Mozart effect was a creation of the popular media and has no compelling scientific backing. But this is not to say that listening to music has no place in pregnancy. In fact, music can have a calming effect on mothers. We also know that music is processed at some level by the unborn baby. For example, two to four day old infants recognise the jingle of a favourite TV programme watched at the end of pregnancy (Hepper, 1991). However, these tunes are soon forgotten.

## ACTIVITIES TO SUPPORT MUSICAL DEVELOPMENT

### 0 to 1 year

Offer musical toys, both traditional instruments (e.g. glockenspiel) as well as toys that make music.
Sing together and encourage children to sing along.
Dance and move together to the music.
Listen to all different types of music.
Bang pots and pans, fill plastic jars with rice, beans or metal bolts, or find other things that make noise and use them as percussion instruments.

### 1 to 3 years

Adapt tunes and songs that you are already know using silly words.
Sing your favourite songs again and again.
Play guess the tune – hum a tune and have your children guess what it is.
Play hand clapping games which have a song and a repeated clapping pattern (you can find examples online).
Watch live musical performances, even if it's just buskers on the street.
Listen to music and do accompanying movements – e.g. falling motion when listening to a descending scale, marching to strong rhythms, etc.
Play copy the rhythm; you model a rhythm and ask your child to copy it.

**4 year olds**

Use ribbon sticks or scarves to move to music, or a parachute if you have one.

Give your child a harmonica to play.

Tap sticks along to the rhythm of a song.

Play a keep the rhythm game – you both tap out a beat, and then try to follow the beat when you speak. Choose a topic such as 'full name'; then you both have to try to state your full name while speaking the syllables to the beat.

Allow free listening time, where your child can choose the music she listens to and can control which song is playing.

ACTIVITIES TO ENCOURAGE LISTENING SKILLS

Fill a box with things that make different types of noises. Ask your child, 'What do I have inside my box?' For each thing taken out, your child needs to find words to describe the noise.

Find a really noisy object. Try to pass it between you and your child without making a noise. Or have your child close her eyes and put the object in front of her. Try to take it, without her hearing you do it.

Listen to a sound fade away – put your hand up when you can't hear it any longer.

Take out the paints or markers and paint or draw a representation of how the music makes you feel.

## Frequently asked questions – music and young children

### Why do children love music?

Researchers are intrigued by babies' love for music. The observation that five month old infants move in time, both to music and to regular rhythms, suggests an evolutionary importance. However, it's not clear what advantage music might offer. Some have suggested that a good sense of rhythm may have been advantageous in mating rituals involving dance (Miller, 2000). While this argument is not particularly compelling, it is clear that moving to music makes children happy. In fact, research has shown that the better a young child can match her movements to the beat of the music, the more fun she appears to be having (Zentner & Eerola, 2010). There is also a social component to this. Some experiments have demonstrated that infants bounced around in time, rather than out of time, with the movements of an adult are kinder to the adult subsequently. For example, they are more likely to hand over an object that the adult has pretended to drop, such as a piece of paper (Cirelli, Einarson, & Trainor, 2014).

While it's not clear why children love music so much, the key message to parents is to provide lots of opportunities for silly messing around with music. There's nothing more encouraging to children than to see an adult dancing, or playing an instrument alongside them. Listening to music together also provides great bonding and learning opportunities. Move up on your toes when the pitch in the music is high and down on the ground when it's low. Encourage your child to take the lead. Clap and move to a prominent beat. Do whatever comes naturally.

### Will my child always love music?

It's a good idea to enjoy musical games with young children, as research shows the freestyle bopping stage doesn't last long. Large scale studies show that spontaneously moving about to music declines when children get older. When entering school, children start to spend more time listening to music rather than moving around to it. They may also begin more formal learning with musical instruments or organised dance (Moog, 1976).

### I have read that having music lessons will make my child smarter; is this true?

There are a number of benefits that children will gain from the formal learning of an instrument or singing. Music lessons involve extended periods of sustained concentration, along with the learning and daily reading of musical notation and musical theory. There is also the discipline involved in practising and the detailed technique and physical mastery required. However, there is currently no consistent evidence that learning an instrument or having singing lessons will impact upon your child's IQ.

## Is there a certain type of music/sound that will comfort my young child?

Young children prefer to hear the unaccompanied voice of their mother singing (Ilari & Sundara, 2009). However, early studies suggested that young children when trying to fall asleep prefer to hear any noise rather than no noise at all. Experimenters played young children (both new-borns and preschoolers) a metronome (which ticks a steady beat), the sound of a heartbeat and a lullaby. All of these were equally effective and children fell asleep significantly faster when played any one of them compared to hearing nothing at all (Brackbill, Adams, Crowell, & Gray, 1966).

## Why do young children enjoy lullabies?

Some researchers have suggested that children are drawn to sung lullabies because of the positive emotions that are conveyed (Trainor, 1996). No doubt this has an adaptive function, where the child is drawn to figures who provide safety, protection and caring. Singing can also calm down an agitated infant (Shenfield, Trehub, & Nakata, 2003).

## Can my child start learning an instrument at the age of four?

Some children who have high levels of manual coordination, good concentration and long attention spans can start learning a string instrument or the piano from the age of four. However, in most cases this is considered too early. If you do decide to start lessons at this age, it can be helpful to sit in so you know what your child is learning and you can help to guide practice.

## How can you motivate children to practise their instrument?

At this young age, practice should be fun and children should not be pressured into spending too much time at an instrument that they are not enjoying. When children turn six, and you are trying to encourage regular practice, a few things can help. Allowing a child to choose an instrument she enjoys may make practice less of a chore. It may also help if the child is part of a group that meets regularly to play the instrument together.

## Is my child too young to begin singing lessons?

Most vocal professionals will recommend that individual singing lessons begin after the age of 11 or for a boy after he has gone through puberty. However, often this can depend upon the maturity of an individual child and her desire to be formally taught.

## Can playing an instrument improve my child's motor skills?

Physical coordination and dexterity can be improved though the playing of percussion instruments. Hitting a drum with two sticks, just one of many possible percussive activities, can encourage two handed coordination. Most children are able to hit with both hands together from age two onwards. Practice with drumming will improve hand–eye coordination, manual speed and awareness of rhythm.

## How can I encourage my children to like all kinds of music and not just pop?

When reaching preschool age, children initially show a liking for most types of music, which includes both popular and classical pieces. Research shows that in general, preferences move away from classical towards pop as children enter school. This tendency can be softened when special measures are undertaken to increase children's awareness of and exposure to classical music, such as playing classical recordings and instruments in the home (Peery & Peery, 2014).

## Resources

Brackbill, Y., Adams, G., Crowell, D., & Gray, L. (1966). Arousal level in neonates and preschool children under continuous auditory stimulation. *Journal of Experimental Child Psychology, 4*, 178–188.

Cirelli, L. K., Einarson, K. M., & Trainor, L. J. (2014). Interpersonal synchrony increases prosocial behavior in infants. *Developmental Science, 17*(6), 1003–1011. http://doi.org/10.1111/desc.12193

Hallam, S. (2010). The power of music: Its impact on the intellectual, social and personal development of children and young people. *International Journal of Music Education, 28*(3), 269–289. http://doi.org/10.1177/0255761410370658

Hepper, P. G. (1991). An examination of fetal learning before and after birth. *Irish Journal of Psychology, 12*(2), 95–107. http://doi.org/10.1080/03033910.1991.10557830

Ilari, B., & Sundara, M. (2009). Music listening preferences in early life. *Journal of Research in Music Education, 56*(4), 357–369.

Kirschner, S., & Tomasello, M. (2010). Joint music making promotes prosocial behavior in 4-year-old children. *Evolution and Human Behavior, 31*(5), 354–364. http://doi.org/10.1016/j.evolhumbehav.2010.04.004

Miller, G. F. (2000). Evolution of human music through sexual selection. In N. L. Wallin, B. Merker, & S. Brown, Eds. *The Origins of Music.* Cambridge, MA: MIT Press.

Moffitt, T. E., Arseneault, L., Belsky, D., Dickson, N., Hancox, R. J., Harrington, H., et al. (2011). A gradient of childhood self-control predicts health, wealth, and public safety. *Proceedings of the National Academy of Sciences of the United States of America, 108*(7), 2693–2698. http://doi.org/10.1073/pnas.1010076108

Moog, H. (1976). The development of musical experience in children of pre-school age. *Psychology of Music, 4*(2), 38–45. http://doi.org/10.1177/0305735691192001

Peery, C., & Peery, I. (2014). Effects of exposure to classical music on the musical preferences of preschool children. *Journal of Research in Music Education, 34*(1), 24–33.

Rauscher, F., Shaw, G., & Ky, K. (1993). Music and spatial task performance. *Nature, 365,* 611.

Shenfield, T., Trehub, S. E., & Nakata, T. (2003). Maternal singing modulates infant arousal. *Psychology of Music, 31*(4), 365–375. http://doi.org/10.1177/0305735603314002

St Clair-Thompson, H. L., & Gathercole, S. E. (2006). Executive functions and achievements in school: Shifting, updating, inhibition, and working memory. *Quarterly Journal of Experimental Psychology, 59*(4), 745–759. http://doi.org/10.1080/17470210500162854

Trainor, L. J. (1996). Infant preferences for infant-directed versus noninfant-directed playsongs and lullabies. *Infant Behavior and Development, 19*(1), 83–92. http://doi.org/10.1016/S0163-6383(96)90046-6

Zentner, M., & Eerola, T. (2010). Rhythmic engagement with music in infancy. *Proceedings of the National Academy of Sciences of the United States of America, 107*(13), 5768–5773. http://doi.org/10.1073/pnas.1000121107

Becky Cameron

# 11   Does my child have ADHD?

**Parent post – ADHD**

*I'm wondering whether our four year old boy has ADHD. He has always been a tricky child. As a baby he was constantly crying or fussing. He started walking at the age of ten months and hasn't stopped moving since. As a toddler, I could never leave him alone, he was always getting into trouble. Now, as a four year old, things are even more difficult. He only sleeps for short periods of time and won't sit still for long, even to watch TV. Time outs don't work. Whenever we put him in his room, he destroys it.*

*At preschool, he has no friends and is often involved in fights with other children. Once we were asked to keep him at home for a few days, but it made no difference. In fact, he seemed to enjoy it. The whole family is very stressed out, and nobody knows what to do. We really need some help.*

Most toddlers are frequently restless, easily excitable, and find it difficult to concentrate. At two and three this is typical behaviour, but when does it become worrisome? What if your three year old is also defiant and challenging? Understanding your child's underlying difficulties, as well as having a go at tried and tested approaches, can help. The good news is that literature and practical support are available for parents of children with attention and hyperactivity difficulties.

## Attention deficit hyperactivity disorder (ADHD) – subtypes and how to recognise them

More and more children are being referred for the evaluation and treatment of ADHD symptoms. While ADHD is one of the most commonly diagnosed childhood mental health disorders, it is also very controversial. Some experts argue it is overdiagnosed, while others claim underdiagnosis. Also problematic is the age at which ADHD should be diagnosed. Many clinicians argue that ADHD behaviours are just the extreme end of normal preschool behaviour. Others argue that early diagnosis is key. Whatever the arguments it is clear that preschoolers with ADHD symptoms are more likely to face cognitive and language deficits, as well as greater behavioural and academic problems (Willoughby, Curran, & Costello, 1997).

The *Diagnostic and Statistical Manual* (*DSM*) 5, one popular set of criteria used to diagnose developmental disorders, recognises three different types of ADHD. There is the predominantly inattentive type and the predominantly hyperactive-impulsive type, while some children have a combination of the two, known as the combined type. While all four year olds will have some of the symptoms listed, children with ADHD find normal life difficult. Their symptoms are severe enough to require professional attention. Below are some typical vignettes.

### Parent post – inattentive ADHD?

*Our little girl has always been a bit of a sit-and-watcher. At playgroup she is happy for others to take the lead, and just looks on while they go about their activities. Sometimes she will join in, but only if encouraged. Since she has started preschool, the reports always say 'Lucy is a bit of a dreamer'. She doesn't really pay attention at circle time and when asked a question, it always has to be repeated. She has always been eager to please everyone, and has never got into any trouble. However, we are worried about how she will cope when starting school. She doesn't show any interest in properly learning the alphabet, although she can count to ten. She also doesn't seem to remember what happened the day before, yet she will come up with detailed memories of something that happened last year. Lucy is happiest when wandering around, picking up things to play with here and there. We're worried how well she will cope with the restrictions of the classroom.*

## Features of the inattentive type of ADHD

### *The development of focused attention*

At preschool age, it is as typical to see children who concentrate well as it is to see children with no sustained attention whatsoever. While some will sit still for a long time, others will start squirming from the five minute mark, or may reject an activity entirely. At this age, it is difficult to know whether poor concentration is just part of normal development or will be problematic.

It is clear that exerting focused attention requires a great deal of effort for some children. Your child's ability to concentrate and block out distractions will be related to a number of other features, such as the knowledge that she has already acquired, and her general level of cognitive development. In a practical example of this, children who understand more about what is happening in a TV show will watch it for longer. Not only does following the plot or content of a TV programme make it more interesting; children who have a high general ability will also often have higher levels of attention or concentration. In general, a child's ability to demonstrate focused attention will expand rapidly from the age of 2.5 to 4.5 years (Ruff & Lawson, 1990) and will continue to grow into the early school years. Over the preschool years, children will become more focused in their movements, and those not specifically related to accomplishing a goal will fall away.

### *Inattention*

Children with ADHD have more difficulty concentrating than their peers. If they try very hard, these children may hold their attention for short periods of time. However, children with ADHD will find this exhausting and soon become worn out. This explains why they often make a good start to an activity, but don't finish. They may also start the day well, but grow tired and irritable by the afternoon. Children with inattentive ADHD will need close supervision to get things done. For example, when asked to get dressed, children with ADHD may find a large number of distraction activities. This will be particularly true if they find what they are supposed to do difficult or boring.

Some features of children with the inattentive type of ADHD are:

• frequently not completing tasks
• being very disorganised and having difficulties following the sequence of tasks (e.g. remembering to put pants on before trousers)
• often daydreaming.

## Parent post – hyperactive and impulsive ADHD

*My three year old's tantrums are really intense. They are much stronger and more out of control than those of other three year olds I know. They also seem to come out of nowhere. Trying to get him out of the door is a nightmare. I have to put him in a spot where there is nothing to distract him, and it still takes him forever to get ready. I almost always have to end up helping him. When we go on play dates, he runs around the house and is impossible to control. I often have to replace toys that he has destroyed on a whim. I'm worried that, rather than settling down, he is getting worse as he gets older.*

## Features of the hyperactive-impulsive type of ADHD

Ask many parents what an ADHD child looks like, and they will describe a child who can't sit still. At one time hyperactivity was considered to be an essential feature of the diagnosis and at the heart of ADHD. However, careful study showed that while most children with ADHD are more restless or fidgety than others, they are not all overactive. For example, they may demonstrate primarily inattentive features and be diagnosed with the inattentive type of ADHD (see last parent post).

Although the number of inattentive diagnoses is rising, it is still the hyperactive-impulsive type which makes up the majority of children with ADHD. These children are indeed always on the go. Sometimes they cannot remain still even for a moment. They may also have great difficulty stopping and thinking before they act. This means that they will do the first thing that comes into their head, even if this means running in front of a car. They may also be very loud and boisterous and find quiet activities very difficult. Children with hyperactive-impulsive ADHD sometimes repeatedly make loud noises, like always repeating the brmm brmm of a car. Such noises may become a habit, and they may not even be aware that they are making them. While they may stop the noise for a short time if requested, they will start again soon after, often without even noticing.

### *Impulsivity*

Impulsivity refers to acting reflexively or without thinking. Children with ADHD will often act on a whim or as a result of the smallest encouragement from another child. They may even destroy toys that they enjoy. They can also be big risk takers and for this reason may get themselves into trouble or accidents and may be a frequent visitor at the hospital or doctor's surgery. Children with ADHD may also want to touch everything and everyone. This may be very unpopular with other children who do not want to be touched. It may also be difficult when out shopping where things may get easily damaged or broken.

### *Hyperactivity*

Preschool children are naturally restless and fidgety. They make a lot of movements that have no particular goal but go along with the main action they are performing. So, for example, while a young child is squeezing a ball in one hand, the other hand makes a similar motion. When in parallel, these are called mirror movements. In later childhood there are a few what are called 'overflow' movements, for example sticking out a tongue when performing a difficult motor activity. As the school years begin, the frequency of unnecessary movements decreases as control mechanisms in the brain mature. Children with a diagnosis of ADHD may be more likely to retain some overflow movements (such as moving the tongue when writing), demonstrating an inefficiency of the motor networks in the brain.

Hyperactivity in children with ADHD may range from having occasional feelings of restlessness to being 'driven by a motor', where a child never walks but always runs and climbs onto everything. This is often most extreme in the early years, as even the most active children usually slow down over time. In fact, some children with hyperactive-impulsive ADHD become underactive in later years. At this point, parents complain that their child with ADHD prefers to sit on the sofa watching TV or playing video games and won't engage in other activities.

## Features across all children with ADHD

Irrespective of subtype, there are a few areas where all children with ADHD face difficulties. For example, many children with ADHD can be hard on themselves and may have **low self-esteem.** They may overtly say things such as 'I'm stupid' or 'I have no friends'; alternatively, they may try to hide their feelings of inadequacy by bragging or adopting a *know it all* attitude.

Children with ADHD perform significantly below their peers on tasks requiring the use of executive function skills. The executive functions are our higher level thinking skills and include our working memory (see next page) as well as our abilities to control our attention and inhibit our impulses. Specifically, children with ADHD find it difficult to inhibit a familiar or automatic response, plan ahead or use their verbal or spatial working memory.

Related to the poor concentration and forgetfulness of some children with ADHD is a low functioning **working memory**. Working memory is the system that controls attention and stores information while it is being used. It is essential for maintaining focused behaviour and used in most practical situations. For example, working memory is required when reasoning out a problem or deciding a next course of action. Working memory is also necessary for many school-based activities, such as answering questions about a story just read or following the thread of a plot. Children with ADHD consistently show weaknesses in the amount of information they can hold in their working memories (Kasper, Alderson, & Hudec, 2012).

Children with ADHD also have great difficulty working towards delayed rewards. Both types of ADHD are associated with what is known as **poor incentive motivation**. Scientists think this is because of differences in the neurotransmitter system related to rewards. For this reason, in children with ADHD, things like star charts (where points for wanted behaviour add up to a desired reward) may often be ineffective. A quick fix, where gratification is available immediately, will always be more appealing. Television, video games, playing with a new toy, or any available desirable activity, will provide strong temptation for a child with ADHD. Working with these immediate rewards may be more effective.

## Friendships in children with ADHD

It is an unfortunate reality that many children with ADHD struggle with making and keeping friends. Many of these children have **clumsy social skills** and may experience a good deal of social rejection. Children with ADHD often have difficulty appraising a social situation and may show behaviour that is overzealous, insensitive, aggressive or inflexible. These children may be overly intrusive or disruptive and may not understand how their behaviour affects other children. Children with ADHD can often have difficulties learning the skills to make friends and lack the ability to fit in with the children around them. Research shows that children with the inattentive type of ADHD can be neglected. This means they are often ignored or left out of the social networks of their peers, and may spend a lot of time playing by themselves. This is in contrast to children with the hyperactive element of ADHD, who can be actively rejected by peers (Wheeler & Caryn, 1994). This can sometimes be made worse by **defiant behaviour**, which is found more often in the hyperactive-impulsive type of ADHD. A defiant child resists authority and is very difficult to discipline. Other young children can be sensitive to children who are always in trouble and may want to keep their distance.

## Poor coping behaviours

Children with ADHD often struggle with feelings of low self-esteem, as they judge themselves negatively in comparison to their peer group. These feelings can produce coping behaviours which can make existing problems worse. For example, many children with ADHD use deflecting behaviours. The idea here is that attention is focused on a behaviour they choose, rather than one that might further lower their self-esteem. For example, a child may act out in class to deflect from poor social or academic skills. While adults may become frustrated and want to make critical comments to an ADHD child, in fact this will only further lower self-esteem and may exacerbate unwanted behaviours. Although no doubt difficult at times, happy feelings and affection may be most helpful in getting cooperation from a child with ADHD. Many of the undesirable behaviours seen in children with ADHD, such as rejecting or avoiding homework or school, cheating, being aggressive or bullying, are related to feelings of low self-worth.

---

### Parent post – girls and ADHD

*My five year old daughter has recently been diagnosed with ADHD. She is very chatty, has poor impulse control and is always on the go. She gets up at 6 and is still going at 10 in the evening. She also has poor social skills. When we went to see her doctor, she said that she doesn't like to medicate girls as they often 'grow out of it'. I would love to know if this follows the general medical opinion. As we have been really struggling as a family, I thought that some medication might help us to get on a bit better.*

---

## Attention difficulties in girls

It's not surprising that ADHD is typically thought of as a boys' thing. There are about three times as many boys as girls with ADHD symptoms in the general population. However, when considering children with a clinical diagnosis of ADHD, this ratio rises to almost ten boys to one girl (Biederman et al., 2002). Given these numbers, it's not surprising that our understanding of ADHD comes mostly from males. Also, considering the differences in sex ratio between treated and untreated populations, we might guess that girls with ADHD are generating less attention, and causing fewer problems, than their male ADHD counterparts. It's not clear whether girls are referred for clinical services less often, or whether their symptoms are not being recognised as ADHD by medical professionals. Alternatively, it may be both.

There is also no clear picture of sex differences in ADHD. While some studies suggest girls are more often diagnosed with the inattentive form of ADHD, others suggest very few symptom differences between girls and boys. There is no evidence suggesting girls with ADHD are more likely to grow out of it. There is, however, some suggestion that later in life girls with ADHD may be more prone to anxiety and depression (Quinn, 2005) and at greater risk for eating disorders (Biederman et al., 2007).

While girls and boys with ADHD have similar symptoms, girls may suffer more from peer rejection. Girl friendship groups are often based on talking, while boy friendships can be more activity based. This can disadvantage girls who have hyperactive ADHD, as their activity profile does not fit into the social parameters of girl only friendship groups.

## What causes ADHD?

It was once assumed that the source of a child's anti-social behaviour could be traced back to poor parenting. However, we now know much better. Who we are is the result of a complex set of interacting factors coming from both our genes and the environment. While parenting is an influential factor, it is very difficult to say that a certain parenting behaviour causes a particular outcome.

ADHD is understood not as the result of a single factor, but as related to a combination of risk factors, some inherited, some not. For example, a child will be at greater risk if she has a biological relative with ADHD, experiences extreme early adversity, is low birth weight or is born prematurely. However, no *one* factor will definitively result in ADHD. The disorder appears to be polygenetic, which means a number of different genes are implicated. It is familial, meaning it is more common within families, and heritable, meaning it is at least partially explained through variations in the genetic code passed to us from our family.

ADHD is a neurodevelopmental disorder (similar to autism spectrum disorder, Down syndrome and dyslexia, amongst others), meaning that the child's brain has not followed the typical pathway of development. The generally accepted hypothesis is that in ADHD the brain's chemical messengers (neurotransmitters) are not moving properly. Specifically, the regulation of dopamine is dysfunctional. This deficit is related to poor levels of executive function (see p. 133) and inadequate control of attention in the brain. The dopamine deficit hypothesis of ADHD explains the prescribing of the medication methylphenidate (Ritalin), as it allows dopamine to be more available in the brain. The taking of drugs such as Ritalin is related to positive behavioural changes in children with ADHD, such as increased levels of attention.

### TIPS FOR SUPPORTING CHILDREN WITH ADHD

**Improving low self-esteem:** Children with ADHD can often have low self-esteem. These troubling feelings can underlie defiant behaviours or unwillingness to tackle challenges and can initiate and support a cycle of attempting and achieving little.

Parents can help to provide a boost in self-esteem. The first step is to look at our child's individual set of strengths and weaknesses. In this way, we can build on areas of strength and sensitively encourage improvement on weaknesses. Overall, we can make the most positive difference through obviously enjoying our child's company/sense of humour/observations. We can give **positive love and attention** at every opportunity. In particular, putting aside **one on one time**, without distractions, will make our child feel special, worthy and loved. A **sense of belonging**, whether as part of a family unit, school, religion, neighbourhood, nationality or culture, can also boost self-esteem. So will being given **responsibility** for important tasks, such as carrying the keys to the car, holding the tickets for the show or similar. The feeling of being in control through making one's own choices, such as choosing clothing or play activities, can also help to build feelings of self-worth.

## Frequently asked questions – ADHD

**I have heard that children with ADHD are more likely to continue bed wetting later than other children. Is this true?**

Yes, there is evidence to suggest that young children who demonstrate symptoms of ADHD will also wet the bed, known as enuresis. This appears to be quite common in children with ADHD at age eight, declining over time to age 11 (Shreeram et al., 2009).

**Are children with ADHD more likely to have night terrors and sleep walk?**

In general, children with the hyperactive form of ADHD are more likely to have sleep disturbances, such as restless leg syndrome and sleep related breathing disorders. They are also more likely to experience sleepwalking and night terrors, although this link is not as firmly established.

## Are children with ADHD more likely to have other developmental disorders?

It is often the case that developmental disorders or difficulties are more likely to occur together. Conditions that occur more commonly in young people with ADHD are dyslexia, oppositional defiant disorder, conduct disorder, autism spectrum disorder, depression, anxiety disorder, obsessive-compulsive disorder and bipolar disorder.

## Are girls more likely to be diagnosed with the inattentive type of ADHD?

The hyperactive-impulsive type of ADHD is three times more common in boys than in girls. Clinicians see six times more boys than girls with this type of ADHD, likely because the hyperactive behaviour is disruptive and therefore help is sought. Girls who are ultimately diagnosed are more likely to present with the inattentive type. However, surveys indicate that ADHD boys demonstrate a similar level of inattention and ADHD girls can frequently be hyperactive. Interestingly, hyperactivity in girls does not generate the same level of clinical attention.

## Is there a specific test to diagnose ADHD?

There is no one definitive test for ADHD. Instead, an assessment is made through a combination of tests. Typically, there will be an interview with the main caregiver(s) and teacher. These individuals will often be asked to complete a number of scales. These will likely include a parent rating scale (which can monitor the success of any intervention), an attention span test, a classroom behaviour test and further tests covering the full span of key behaviours related to a diagnosis of ADHD.

## Resources

Biederman, J., Ball, S. W., Monuteaux, M. C., Surman, C. B., Johnson, J. L., & Zeitlin, S. (2007). Are girls with ADHD at risk for eating disorders? Results from a controlled, five-year prospective study. *Journal of Developmental and*

*Behavioral Pediatrics: JDBP*, *28*(4), 302–307. http://doi.org/10.1097/DBP. 0b013e3180327917

Biederman, J., Mick, E., Faraone, S. V., Braaten, E., Doyle, A., Spencer, T., et al. (2002). Influence of gender on attention deficit hyperactivity disorder in children referred to a psychiatric clinic. *American Journal of Psychiatry*, *159*(1), 36–42. http://doi.org/10.1176/appi.ajp.159.1.36

Kasper, L. J., Alderson, R. M., & Hudec, K. L. (2012). Moderators of working memory deficits in children with attention-deficit/hyperactivity disorder (ADHD): A meta-analytic review. *Clinical Psychology Review*, *32*(7), 605–617. http://doi.org/10.1016/j.cpr.2012.07.001

Quinn, P. O. (2005). Treating adolescent girls and women with ADHD: Gender-specific issues. *Journal of Clinical Psychology*, *61*(5), 579–587. http://doi.org/10.1002/jclp.20121

Ruff, H. A., & Lawson, K. R. (1990). Development of sustained, focused attention in young children during free play. *Developmental Psychology*, *26*(1), 85–93. http://doi.org/10.1037/0012-1649.26.1.85

Shreeram, S., Jian-Ping, H., Kalaydjian, A., Brothers, S., & Merikangas, K. (2009). Prevalence of enuresis and its association with attention-deficit/hyperactivity disorder among US children: Results from a nationally representative study. *Journal of the American Academy of Child and Adolescent Psychiatry*, *48*(1), 35–41. http://doi.org/10.1097/CHI.0b013e318190045c.Prevalence

Wheeler, J., & Caryn, L. (1994). The social functioning of children with ADD with hyperactivity and ADD without hyperactivity: A comparison of their peer relations and social deficits. *Journal of Emotional and Behavioral Disorders*, *2*(1), 2–12.

Willoughby, M. T., Curran, P. J., & Costello, E. J. (1997). Implications of early versus late onset of attention-deficit/hyperactivity disorder symptoms. *Journal of the American Academy of Child and Adolescent Psychiatry*, *39*(12), 1512–1519. http://doi.org/10.1097/00004583-200012000-00013

Becky Cameron

# 12 How can I help my child do well, without being pushy?

## Parent post – am I being pushy?

*My daughter is just coming up to three, and already knows her numbers to 50. She also knows all of the letters of the alphabet, shapes and colours etc. and can recognise many common words. While I've enjoyed teaching her these things, I'm worried that I'm being pushy. What if, when she gets to school, she is bored because she knows it already? I want her to enjoy learning, not be resentful of studying because I've been pushing her too hard. How can I help her to do well, without being a pushy parent?*

Supporting our children to be happy, thriving, successful individuals is a primary goal for most parents. Parenting gurus know this and have produced a book for pretty much every parenting topic out there, from weaning your child and introducing solids, to choosing the best university. While some parents will feel happy to leave the educating to teachers, other parents will want to support learning at home. Whatever your feelings, confidence with a few basic skills will make the transition to school easier. Outlined below are some key areas where you can help your child to be school ready without being a pushy parent.

## Getting ready for school

1   **Self-care**
    Self-care is the ability for your child to attend to her own basic day to day needs. This includes being able to look after herself in the toilet and to dress and undress, including buttoning buttons and putting on shoes. Also important is how to deal with mealtimes, getting ready for school

and going to bed. Most children will learn these routines through regular practice. In school, being able to change for sports and put on coats and outdoor clothing independently means children will feel secure in their ability to fit into the school routine.

## 2   Making friends

Having friends benefits your child, even when she is very young. The ability for a preschooler to maintain friendships demonstrates a good level of social and emotional understanding and skill. Not surprisingly, preschool children with friends are more pro-social and are more likely to play or undertake projects with others. They are also less aggressive. When they play with their friends, their play is more elaborate and collaborative than with non-friends (Blair et al., 2014). Also, preschool friends can, in some cases, provide support in the transition to school.

Despite the many benefits, early friendships are considered less important than those formed in the school years. Early years' friendships are often more temporary and are based around shared activity and play. However, real emotional bonds do develop and parents sometimes report sadness and loneliness where a close friendship has ended (Blair et al., 2014).

## 3   Self-control

Central to success in school is our child's ability to manage her emotions and control her behaviour. Often children who are young in the year, or simply young in terms of their development, have difficulties with this and fitting into the classroom. There are a huge number of expectations from children at school, for example, following the routines of the day, coping with and responding to teachers' expectations and reprimands, following instructions as well as interacting appropriately with others during class time. All of them demand heavy amounts of self-control.

### Parent post – the marshmallow experiment

*I'd like to know what the marshmallow experiment is all about and why there is such a big fuss around delayed gratification. I've heard it's the most important thing in predicting academic achievement in children, but I don't really understand why.*

**4    Delay of gratification**

So how can eating sweets help your child to achieve her goals and live out her dreams? Well, it's not actually the eating of sweets that's important. It's the *delaying* of that pleasure. Most children would eat a sweet within easy reach. But what if you offered her the alternative of resisting the sweet, waiting a short while, and in return receiving a much larger reward? Would she be able to resist the temptation of gobbling up what she can see in front of her?

The ability to override reflexive thoughts or responses falls under the category of skills known as the executive functions. As discussed in other sections of this book, the executive functions are related to the prefrontal area of the brain, one of the slowest areas to mature. One of the primary roles of the prefrontal cortex is to regulate what we see, think and feel by recruiting and overriding other areas of the brain. Self-control and other executive functions, such as reasoning and planning, are not well developed in the preschool years. However, by the fourth year, children vary greatly in their ability to control their more basic reflexive actions. Part of your child being school-ready involves her ability to override these impulses. Providing opportunities where your child can work towards advantageous delayed rewards can offer good practice, which will transfer well to the classroom.

**5    Paying attention**

Narrowing attention, to focus on what is important, is essential for learning to take place. Your child's ability to selectively pay attention develops over early childhood and is in part driven by the ability to block out information that is irrelevant or distracting. In both infancy and the early years, it's pretty obvious when children are paying close attention. Usually they will have an intense expression on their face and won't move their bodies much. When concentrating hard, both babies and older children are able to block out sounds and images that may distract them. The main difference that separates infants from children here is the length of time for which they can maintain their attention. By age four, children should be able to hold their attention across short structured classroom tasks. Schools will be sensitive to this and will provide longer periods for quiet concentration as children get older.

**6    Working memory**

The ability to hold, or hold and update, information for short periods of time is known as short term or working memory. Your child will be able to hold information over a delay at around six months, and will gradually increase her capacity. Four year olds can usually recall, in the correct order, around two to three images that have been recently presented. At age 12 this will be closer to six (Gathercole, 1998). The ability to update information that is being held in memory is a more advanced skill and develops at around the age of two and improves over the preschool period.

## 7   Response inhibition

The ability for young children to stop themselves from doing something, known as response inhibition, is a heavily researched area. As mentioned above, the famous *marshmallow experiment* tested how long pre-schoolers could delay getting a reward in order to be given a bigger one (Mischel, Ebbesen, & Zeiss, 1972). Simpler experiments are also available and test similar capabilities in younger children. In one example, a child reaches out for a toy and mum says, 'Don't'. The experimenters then watch to see how many children pull a hand back and stop themselves mid-action. On average, just under 50 per cent of two year olds do this, with more than half complying at the age of three (Kochanska, Tjebkes, & Forman, 1998).

Experiments testing the ability to delay gratification most commonly use a waiting or choice setup. In the waiting experiments, the child is shown two desirable treats. She can either wait the total time required and get both, or she can ring the bell at any point and have just one. While on average about half of two year olds are able to wait 20 seconds without ringing the bell, the average three year old can wait for *one whole minute*! The good news is that a typical four year old can usually wait for around five minutes to obtain the two treats (Carlson, 2005).

In the choice experiments, preschoolers can choose between a small reward now and a larger reward later. In one example, three year olds chose the immediate option of one sticker over waiting for a reward of three. However, this changed when the children turned four. At this age, children were able to reason out the greater value of the delayed reward and wait the required time (Lemmon & Moore, 2007).

In summary, parents can expect some self-control in place by the age of three, even if there hasn't been much at age two. By four, you can definitely hope and expect that your child will be able to use reasoning to delay her rewards. The development of these higher order skills is perfectly timed for entry to school.

## Why is denying temptation important?

While it's clearly a good thing to have a hold on our impulses, is it really that important? Actually, the ability to delay instant gratification, and work for long term goals, is the foundation to academic success. For example, there is a large amount of self-discipline involved in studying. When in school we are expected to spend hours working at a desk, avoiding the temptation of immediate and more interesting distractions. In return, we may have the delayed reward of good grades or, in the really long term, a job in the area of our interests. With this in mind, it may not be that surprising that the outcomes from the marshmallow experiment, in terms of the number of seconds that each child waited, have since been found to predict SAT score outcomes as well as social and emotional coping in adolescence (Shoda, Mischel, & Peake, 1990).

Of course, all temptations are not equal. While in some cases impulses may be resisted through logical reasoning, in other situations different strategies, such as physically removing oneself from the situation, may be required. In explaining the systems at play, the authors of the marshmallow experiment have suggested the existence of two interacting systems – hot and cool. The cool system, also termed the *know* system, is about reasoned thought, while the hot, or *go*, system is about emotional or unconditional responding. Needless to say the hot system is dominant in early childhood, while the cool system takes time to develop and relates to brain maturation.

The originators of the marshmallow experiment examined how some children were able to wait out the necessary time to get a larger reward. First of all, they found that children in general waited longer when they couldn't see either the immediate or the delayed reward. Secondly, those children who were the best waiters often sang to themselves or played games. Essentially, those who were better able to distract themselves waited the longest. The message for encouraging self-control is to remove temptations from sight and support children in developing strategies to spend time on their own without structured tasks or adult direction.

## Can we teach self-control?

There have been a number of programmes developed to promote self-control in young children. Not surprisingly, these have been devised for children who are particularly impulsive, and therefore may not be appropriate for all children. In one extreme example, weighted jackets, which can slow children down, have been suggested for children with impulsivity problems. However, they are not recommended for everyday parenting.

The use of self-talk, where a child narrates what she is doing, can help preschool children to stay on task (see later in this chapter for a practical example). It can also help boost resistance to interference or resistance to temptation (Mischel & Patterson, 1976). In some cases, parents are able to successfully build their child's self-control through the use of a reward system. Rewards are given immediately in the younger years and become delayed as children reach school age. However, a general reliance on rewards for motivating behaviour is not recommended. This can promote externalised thinking, where children value a task only for what it can bring them, rather than internalising moral values associated with pro-social behaviour.

---

### Parent post – summer born boy

*My three year old son is an August baby and he has recently started nursery three days a week. He has found fitting in difficult and comes home tired and emotionally overwhelmed. I'm really worried about how he will cope with starting school in a few months' time. I'm considering asking nursery to keep him on and asking school whether they can delay his entry. It's a difficult one, as he may then stick out as being older than the rest of the class. Do summer born children under-perform compared to their classmates? If so, how long does this last?*

---

## Summer born children and school readiness

Reports in both the UK and the US show, on average, summer born children performing slightly under the rest of their peers in primary school. For example, a review of Key Stage 1 (age 7) performance in Maths and English in the UK found autumn born children did best. Spring born children showed the next best performance, followed by summer borns as the lowest achievers (Sharp, Hutchison, & Whetton, 1995). In a large US cohort studied by the National Institute of Child Health and Human Development (NICHD), children who were older when starting kindergarten made consistently greater academic progress. However, there was no relationship between age of school entry and socio-emotional functioning (Lin & Scott, 2007). Importantly, home environment and family characteristics were also strong determinants of educational outcomes.

Age differences within a school year are related to ability differences in the early years of schooling. However, most studies show this gap lessens over time. Social economic status (SES), special needs status and your child's gender provide a much more consistent predictor of school outcomes.

## Parent post – boys' underperformance

*I've got four older children, and I see the same pattern every time. As they get into school, the boys in the class underperform compared to the girls. Even the boys who are bright, and don't mind revising, don't do as well as the girls of the same ability. I've got a young son just about to start school, and I want to break the trend and see him do well. Why do boys not perform as well as girls? What can I do to help my son do well in school?*

You may have heard that we're having a 'boy crisis'. These headlines followed reports that boys are falling behind girls in all areas of schooling. On average, girls do better than boys, no matter what the subject. For example, in England, at age 16+, more boys than girls fail to get five A*–C grades in their GCSEs. This has puzzled researchers, as girls do not outperform boys on aptitude tests; in fact, on the mental rotation test (where two three dimensional objects need to be compared through mental manipulation), boys generally do better (Voyer, Voyer, & Bryden, 1995). However, there is a difference between these two types of assessment. One-off tests, such as the mental rotation test, require short bursts of concentration and aptitude. Doing well in school requires long term persistence and consistency of performance over time. Also, some suggest the classroom is not suited to the particular learning needs of boys. In other words, there is too much sitting and listening.

## Boys' underperformance at school

Many boys are doing very well at school. Looking at average performance across girls and boys means that a lot of individual performance is hidden. However, it is clear that there is a large group of boys who are underperforming.

There have been a number of suggestions as to why boys are not reaching their full potential in formal learning environments. Some of these are:

- the 'sit still and listen' format of the traditional classroom
- the over-representation of women teachers and other staff in primary schools and thus a lack of male academic role models
- the 'feminisation' of learning and the devaluing of male strengths.

While some parents may find these theories compelling, they are hard to test. More measurable factors that have been suggested are:

*Boys spend less time reading.* They have also been found to generally enjoy reading less than girls (National Literacy Trust, 2012). Surveys such as those undertaken by the National Literacy Trust suggest reading for enjoyment is related to good academic achievement in both girls and boys.

*Boys spend less time doing homework than girls.* Studies suggest that undertaking homework set by teachers is linked to better performance in secondary school. However, in primary school, weaker students can often spend a longer period completing set homework, so this relationship does not necessarily hold true in the younger years.

*Boys' work may be marked down for their unwanted behaviour in class.* When tests are anonymised, boys typically do better.

The following tips, games and activities can be useful in promoting school readiness in your young child.

### TIPS TO HELP YOUR CHILD TO MAKE FRIENDS

In order to teach useful strategies, these friendship scenarios can be modelled using puppets, with a child playing herself. Alternatively, the situations can just be discussed when they occur naturally between siblings.

**What should you say when you want to play with a toy another child is playing with?**

- Can I have a turn?
- Can we swap toys?
- Can I have a go in five minutes? (A five minute timer is often available in preschool/school settings.)

**What should you say when two friends are playing and you would like to join in?**

- Can I play too?
- Suggest getting something that can help with their game – e.g. getting some extra toys.
- Find a role for yourself – e.g. can I be referee?

**How can you make friends with someone you don't know?**

- Say, 'Hi, my name is . . . What's your name? Do you want to play?

### GAMES FOR PROMOTING SELF-REGULATION AND SELF-CONTROL IN YOUR CHILD

All games where it is necessary to follow a set of rules provide an opportunity for children to develop self-control. One study (Tominey & McClelland,

2011) identified a number of preschooler games which were particularly helpful for developing regulation skills. Most of these are traditional games turned slightly on their head. These can easily be played at home.

**Red light, purple light.** One person acts as the stop light at the opposite end from where the other is standing. She holds up coloured circles, which tell the other person what to do. So, for example, red could mean go and purple mean stop and green mean go slowly. Then the meaning of the colours can change around, and the other person has to remember and update the rules.

**Freeze.** Your child dances wildly to music and freezes when the music stops. In this version of the game, she should dance quickly when the music is slow, and dance slowly when the music is fast.

**Sleeping, sleeping, all the children are sleeping.** Your child pretends to sleep while you are singing over and over, 'sleeping, sleeping, all the children are sleeping'. You then give an instruction such as 'and when they woke up they were monkeys!' and the children then jump up immediately and act in character.

**Conducting an orchestra.** You and your child can take turns at being conductor and orchestra. Holding a baton, the conductor makes fast or slow movements, and the orchestra, either you or your child with some noise making device, respond accordingly.

ACTIVITIES USING SELF-TALK TO PROMOTE SELF-REGULATION

In these activities, you model what you are doing and thinking while doing a task. Showing a rational and reasoned thinking process can help your child to think through things in a similar manner. So, for example, getting ready for breakfast:

> So . . . I come into the kitchen and get the cloth to wipe the table; oh it's dry, so I turn on the tap and put the cloth under the water. It's wet now so I can start wiping the table, oh it doesn't take long to do, just a few wipes and I'm done . . .

And so on . . . Once your child gets more used to staying on task, she can just whisper the narration.

Create elaborate scenarios for play with your children and then let them go to it. So, for example, imagine you are on a fishing boat and you need a captain and a passenger. Imagine all of the interactions that might happen: getting lost, crashing into an iceberg, trying to catch a fish and eat it for dinner. Give your children some ideas and then let them extend the story themselves. Encourage them to stay within the confines of their imagined character. What sort of things does a captain or a passenger do/not do? Their ability to interact and respond, with each staying within a role, helps to promote self-regulation and self-control.

## Frequently asked questions – supporting your child's potential

### Is it important for a child to have close friends?

Having friends is a good indication that a child has well developed social skills. If your child does not have friends, she may need support in learning how to make and keep friendships. Earlier in the chapter, some example role playing scenarios were given which might help your child to get the ball rolling. Getting along well with peers will become particularly important when your child starts school. Children without friends may feel lonely and suffer psychologically from perceived peer rejection. However, not all friendships are made equal. For example, friendships vary widely in how the children play together and whether this is pro or anti-social. Also important is how the friends resolve disagreements and whether this consistently involves power assertion by one member of the friendship. Friendships have large differences in terms of time spent together across a range of activities, as well as the emotional quality of the friendship and whether it is characterised by positive or negative feelings.

### Why do young children stick out their tongue when they are thinking/concentrating?

It is not just young children who stick out their tongue when performing an intricate manual task, such as tying shoelaces. Adults can also move their tongue to their lips in a similar type of situation, for example when trying to thread a needle. There is no consensus explanation as to why this happens. Some theories suggest that in the above examples there is too much manual attention being required. This overloads the system and results in the tongue coming out. An alternative suggestion is that the regions of the brain involved in speech and hand movements overlap, and they may both be activated in these tasks.

## Can my two year old control her behaviour?

From the age of about one and a half, most children have a developed system for self-control. At this age your child can most likely stop mid-action and change tack. So, for example, moving towards the cookie jar, your toddler suddenly remembers she is not allowed to take a biscuit without an adult present. She turns around and leaves the room. Of course, this is an ideal situation and many times toddlers will need reminders or may well know what's expected but do exactly as they fancy.

Around the time when toddlers start taking notice of rules and exerting behaviour control (at least some of the time!), you will also see that they are very happy to tell others what they should and should not do. For example, in a nursery setting, children often watch each other's behaviour very closely. For this reason, in group settings, such as early years classrooms, consistent application of the rules can be really important. Children of this age are very sensitive to the perception of fairness.

## What is emotional self-regulation?

The term emotional self-regulation really means the same as the terms we have already been using in this chapter, so impulse control, response inhibition, self-control. They all refer to the ability of children to inhibit their immediate response in favour of behaviour that is socially acceptable.

Emotions are tricky things to define. Essentially, they equip us with a biological (sometimes rapid) response system. They have evolved due to the significant survival advantages they provide. Emotions give us a tool with which to appraise and respond to situations and in many cases are the result of neural activity that occurs in milliseconds (Cole, Martin, & Dennis, 2004). Many of the impulsive reactions of young children will be related to their emotional experience of events.

## Do boys find it particularly difficult to control their impulses?

As a general trend, we see that boys have more difficulty paying attention to particular tasks or, when being addressed, sitting still and more generally stopping themselves from getting into trouble (Matthews,

Ponitz, & Morrison, 2009). Impulsivity can be a trait of attention deficit hyperactivity disorder (ADHD). A much larger proportion of boys than girls is diagnosed with this developmental difficulty.

**Is mindfulness a helpful approach for preschool children?**

There has been an increasing interest in using mindfulness techniques or mindfulness programmes in the early years classroom. In the few published studies, time set aside for each child to adopt a meditative pose and focus on the breath (amongst other mindfulness activities) has been found to be beneficial in lowering impulsive behaviours, amongst other positive outcomes (Flook et al., 2010).

## Resources

Blair, B. L., Perry, N. B., O'Brien, M., Calkins, S. D., Keane, S. P., & Shanahan, L. (2014). The indirect effects of maternal emotion socialization on friendship quality in middle childhood. *Developmental Psychology, 50*(2), 566. http://doi.org/10.1037/a0033532

Carlson, S. M. (2005). Developmentally sensitive measures of executive function in preschool children. *Developmental Neuropsychology, 28*(2), 595–616. http://doi.org/10.1207/s15326942dn2802

Cole, P. M., Martin, S. E., & Dennis, T. A. (2004). Emotion regulation as a scientific construct: Methodological challenges and directions for child development research. *Child Development, 75*(2), 317–333. http://doi.org/10.1111/j.1467-8624.2004.00673.x

Flook, L., Smalley, S. L., Kitil, M. J., Galla, B. M., Kaiser-Greenland, S., Locke, J., Ishijima, E., & Kasari, C. (2010). Effects of mindful awareness practices on executive functions in elementary school children. *Journal of Applied School Psychology, 26*(1), 70–95. http://doi.org/10.1080/15377900903379125

Gathercole, S. E. (1998). The development of memory. *Journal of Child Psychology and Psychiatry, 39*(1), 3–27.

Kochanska, G., Tjebkes, T., & Forman, D. (1998). Children's emerging regulation of conduct: Restraint, compliance, and internalization from infancy to the second year. *Child Development, 69*(5), 1378–1389.

Lemmon, K., & Moore, C. (2007). The development of prudence in the face of varying future rewards. *Developmental Science, 10*(4), 502–511. http://doi.org/10.1111/j.1467-7687.2007.00603.x

Lin, G. G., & Scott, J. G. (2007). Age of entry to kindergarten and children's academic achievement and socioemotional development. *Early Education & Development, 18*(2), 337–368. http://doi.org/10.1016/j.pestbp.2011.02.012.

Matthews, J. S., Ponitz, C. C., & Morrison, F. J. (2009). Early gender differences in self-regulation and academic achievement. *Journal of Educational Psychology*, *101*(3), 689–704. http://doi.org/10.1037/a0014240

Mischel, W., Ebbesen, E. B., & Zeiss, A. R. (1972). Cognitive and attentional mechanisms in delay of gratification. *Journal of Personality and Social Psychology*, *21*(2), 204–218. http://doi.org/10.1037/h0032198

Mischel, W., & Patterson, C. J. (1976). Substantive and structural elements of effective plans for self-control. *Journal of Personality and Social Psychology*, *34*(5), 942–950. http://doi.org/10.1037/0022-3514.34.5.942

National Literacy Trust. (2012). Boys' Reading Commission. Available at www.literacytrust.co.uk

Sharp, C., Hutchison, D., & Whetton, C. (1995). How do season of birth and length of schooling affect children's attainment at key stage 1? Erratum. *Educational Research*, *37*(1), 19. http://doi.org/10.1080/0013188940360201

Shoda, Y., Mischel, W., & Peake, P. K. (1990). Predicting adolescent cognitive and self-regulatory competencies from preschool delay of gratification: Identifying diagnostic conditions. *Developmental Psychology*, *26*(6), 978–986. http://doi.org/10.1037//0012-1649.26.6.978

Tominey, S. L., & McClelland, M. M. (2011). Red light, purple light: Findings from a randomized trial using circle time games to improve behavioral self-regulation in preschool. *Early Education & Development*, *22*(3), 489–519. http://doi.org/10.1080/10409289.2011.574258

Voyer, D., Voyer, S., & Bryden, M. P. (1995). Magnitude of sex differences in spatial abilities: A meta-analysis and consideration of critical variables. *Psychological Bulletin*, *117*(2), 250–270. http://doi.org/10.1037/0033-2909.117.2.250

Becky Cameron

# 13　How can I stop them fighting?

## Parent post – my children don't get on

*I'm in the third year of my degree. I'm studying to be a nurse. I'm at uni a lot during the day, and at night I need to be studying. As the years have gone on, and my children have got older (they are now five and three), they have started bickering constantly about every little thing. Who sits where in the car, who gets which plate, who gets to open the door to the house. It literally doesn't stop. It's tiring, annoying and really quite embarrassing when we are in public. I try not to take sides, and I try to give them each as much attention as I can. However, I worry they aren't getting enough from me and that's why they're acting out. I don't know what to do; I've got to do well at uni for the future of our family. I've never had a close relationship with my siblings, and I really want our children to get along.*

## Sibling relationships

The sibling relationship is unique. In early childhood, siblings play more together than with anyone else. This constant closeness, together with immature emotional regulation, mean relationships can be emotionally intense. A child's feelings towards her brothers and sisters often veer between intense love and feelings of hatred. There is also ambivalence. While friends can be chosen, and friendships can be abandoned, sibling relationships are for life. Even where siblings don't get along, compromises and deals must be struck. Shared resources, such as mum and dad's attention, must be managed.

### Sibling conflict

Conflict between siblings is pretty much a given. By some counts, they occur at a rate of around eight times an hour in childhood. There are a few typical triggers: 1) arguing over a wanted object, 2) an argument over an action that is unwanted (often touching of some sort), or 3) the blocking of a goal of one sibling by another.

Siblings have to share resources and as such there can be a lot of bickering. Only a small proportion of conflict is forceful, hostile or aggressive. When conflict does involve physical fighting, usually, but not always, the older sibling will initiate and win the fight. However, in some cases a younger child may have less control of her impulses and may therefore be the one to commonly behave aggressively. Studies have shown that, in the early years, where there is an older physically aggressive sibling, younger siblings will become more aggressive over time. This is likely due to environmental and genetic factors. Severe aggression in sibling conflict is related to problematic behaviours in at least one of the children more generally.

### The positives of sibling disagreements

While generally unwanted, there are some positive aspects to conflict between younger members of the family. Conflict resolution brings about an opportunity to discuss and reinforce house rules. It can allow for a situation to be reviewed and for ground rules to be established, which can lead to a happier household. A younger child may also come to learn when a rule has been broken and resolve conflict through verbally repeating the rule to an older brother or sister. While the closeness between siblings will create conflict, they also possess an extensive shared history. This can be used to create elaborate and imaginative pretend play. Siblings can also provide emotional support based on intimate long term knowledge of one another.

---

### Parent post – should I get involved?

*My children fight a lot. It drives me crazy and I am always stepping in to sort things out because I can't stand to hear them bickering! My friend told me recently that as long as I keep stepping in, they won't learn how to settle their own differences. Is this true? Their arguments get pretty heated pretty quickly and I'm worried that they might hurt each other. I have two boys aged five and three.*

---

### Stepping in to resolve arguments

Knowing when to step into an argument can be tricky. If anyone is at risk of getting physically hurt, then it is clear that an adult should step in straightaway. Every child has the right to feel safe and protected from harm, particularly in her own home. However, when things aren't physical, your children need space to negotiate their own resolutions. When arguing, a young person has the opportunity to express and defend her own position. She can also learn what works when offering concessions and compromises. Sadly, many arguments between siblings will never get to the negotiation stage. Research suggests most sibling arguments will end in a stand-off or with one sibling submitting to the desires of the other (McGuire, McHale, & Updegraff, 1996).

---

### Parent post – should my children be fighting all the time?

*My children fight all the time; is this normal? My eldest is six and my youngest is three. It feels like every time I walk out of the room, the three year old starts crying because the six year old has hit him or hurt him in some way. I know that sometimes the youngest does things to provoke the older one. I just don't know how to get them to like each other and get on a bit better!*

---

## The nature of sibling relationships

Relationships between siblings vary widely. Psychologists have put the different types of relationships into categories; these are *hostile*, where there is high conflict and low warmth, *affectively intense*, where there is high conflict and high warmth, *harmonious*, where there is high warmth and low conflict, and *uninvolved*, where low warmth and low conflict are observed (McGuire, McHale, & Updegraff, 1996). Of course, many relationships will not fit into these neat categories. Although we may feel the nature of our relationship with our siblings goes through good and bad patches, research shows that the character of these relationships stays pretty much stable over childhood. While it may not be desirable, it's natural that some sibling relationships will be characterised by a higher level of conflict than others.

---

### Parent post – spacing between siblings

*My husband and I are planning our second child and we want to know what the research says in terms of spacing between siblings. How many years between children is the best for encouraging them to get along? And how does gender interact with this? For example, does an older sister get on better with a younger brother?*

### Birth spacing and gender in sibling relationships

Many parents spend a long time thinking about what might be the ideal birth spacing to create a harmonious family. While any two siblings will present their own individual dynamic, there are some documented patterns in sibling relationships. These are *very* general patterns, so we shouldn't give them too much importance. However, in general, a wider gap between siblings is related to more helping behaviours from the older sibling, with more pro-social action and affection. More closely spaced siblings are more likely to quarrel more frequently, show greater antagonism towards each other, and the older sibling is more likely to be dominant (in other words, frequently bossing around her younger sister or brother). The sex of the siblings also plays a role. In general, same sex siblings, particularly sisters, report more affection towards one another (Buhrmester & Furman, 1990).

Often, factors such as birth spacing, and certainly gender, are outside of our control. This shouldn't worry us; in fact, they are not even the most determining characteristics as to how our children will get along. A child's temperament, the behaviour of the mother and the age of the child (sibling relationships usually mellow with age) have all been shown to play a more important role (Stocker, Dunn, & Plomin, 1989).

---

#### Parent post – Daddy's boy

*I know all about not being the favourite child. I grew up with my brother being the angel of the family who could do no wrong. Now, I see my husband treating our little boy the same way. When he is home from work, he makes a special effort to play with him in the backyard. On the weekend, it is all about choosing special activities for them to do together. My daughter, on the other hand, is left at home with me, and most times not even invited. I try to think of special things for us to do together, but I feel bad for her, as I know she misses out on her father's attention. I'm really worried that this is going to affect her in the long term.*

---

## Differential treatment of siblings

You might assume that children growing up together experience the same home environment. However, we now know this isn't necessarily the case. Sibling interactions with parents can be very different, both in terms of how they feel they are treated and how they are actually treated. Most parents will report that each of their children needs them differently. They must therefore be a different parent for each child. In these cases, differential treatment is appropriate and necessary. However, favouritism, where the needs of at least one child are neglected in favour of those of a sibling, can be very detrimental and can impact negatively upon sibling relationships.

Children who perceive themselves to be treated unfairly compared to siblings often express anger or resentment towards their brothers or sisters. This is particularly the case when punishments or distributions of property are felt to be unequal. We sometimes forget that the quality of our children's relationship is also our responsibility. A large part of whether or not our children will get on depends upon the larger family context. Many models of family interaction suggest that the loving bond between parent and child sets the stage for the loving relationship between brothers and sisters. When these bonds are not of equal strength, or the treatment of each child is meaningfully different, problems almost always follow.

---

### Parent post – separation and sibling relationships

*My husband and I have split recently. He lives down the road and we share the care of our two young children equally between us. The situation seems to be working ok; however, I have noticed that the children, aged three and five, seem to be fighting more frequently. I was wondering if this might be related to the stress of the relatively new changes in living circumstances. How does separation or divorce affect the relationships of the children within the family?*

---

## The effect of parental separation/divorce on sibling relationships

Major life events, such as divorce, can often trigger changes in the sibling relationship. During the separation itself, parents can be less available as they deal with their own emotional and practical issues. Particularly in the case of older children, siblings may provide an additional source of emotional support during such turbulent times. The response to traumatic family events heavily depends upon pre-existing relationships. If a sibling relationship was already close, a parental separation can bring the children even closer. However, if the relationship was characterised by rivalry or jealousy, these feelings can be exacerbated. Parental separation most often intensifies the sibling relationship, rather than fundamentally altering it.

---

## Parent post – arrival of a new baby

*I am due to have our second child next month, and am quite concerned that our two year old may feel some jealousy towards her. At the moment she gives the bump lots of cuddles and love; however, when we talk about her sister arriving soon, she becomes quite sulky. What can I do to minimise any rivalry?*

---

A new baby means change. Youngest or only children, in particular, may find themselves dealing with some quite uncomfortable feelings. Older siblings can feel replaced, unwanted or unloved when the newest member arrives. These feelings can result in aggression towards the new baby, attention seeking behaviour or regression (where she goes back to more baby-like behaviours). It may be helpful to show extra love, attention and sensitivity to siblings on the birth of a new baby. Making it clear that all children are loved and valued, and that all needs and wants will be looked after, can help children to relax.

While school and other activities outside the home may distract older children, younger children may have stronger uncomfortable feelings when a new baby arrives. In these cases, parents might teach a sibling how to watch the baby for cues relating to being fed, cuddled, changed, etc. and include her in daily care activities. Constant correcting of the older sibling, or restricting access to the new baby, should be avoided as this can cause feelings of rivalry.

Outlined below are some tips which may be helpful in creating a more harmonious household.

### TIPS ON HOW TO MEDIATE YOUR CHILDREN'S DISPUTES

Mediation is about guiding your children to resolve their own disagreements outside of the heat of battle. You are there to guide the mediation and enforce the rules. While preschoolers may struggle with the process, the foundations can be established, and then can be more fully developed as your children get older.

1   Set the ground rules – what can and can't be said or done in the mediation discussion.
2   Outline the issue(s) at hand – be clear about what the problem is and any influencing factors.
3   Each sibling needs to outline why the other sibling is upset while following the ground rules set in 1.
4   Depending on the age of the children, each sibling needs to suggest a resolution that each member can potentially agree to. Alternatively,

each sibling can propose a list of three, which is then ranked by the other sibling.

5   Only a resolution that can be agreed upon by everyone should be selected.

One of the great benefits of mediation is that children are forced to recognise the opinion and viewpoint of the other child. When mediation techniques are used, children are more likely to discuss their own and others' emotions. This is the case, even when children are too young to really generate ideas of their own.

### TIPS FOR MINIMISING SIBLING CONFLICT

*Use a gripe or grievance book*, where each child can write down the things the other child has done which have been upsetting. This can allow small grievances to be vented without always having to come to an adult.

Rather than comparing one sibling's poor behaviour to another sibling's good behaviour – 'George always hangs his coat up neatly, why can't you?' – *describe the problem and explain what needs to be done* – 'Your coat is on the floor and it should be hung up.'

When one child is misbehaving, avoid giving your attention to the misbehaviour. If your littlest child has hit your eldest, *lavish your attention on the child that has been hurt*, giving kisses and cuddles or an ice pack as appropriate.

*Avoid using negative labels.* So, for example, don't label an older sibling as behaving like a bully, rather remind her: 'You know how to get what you want without hitting your sister.'

*Things not to say to siblings who are fighting* – 'Stop it now!' Both children think, if I stop now, he'll/she'll win, so nothing changes.

'Who started it?' No one is going to own up to starting the fight and so that doesn't achieve anything.

'You two are always fighting.' Again, both children think the other child started it, and this doesn't move anything forward in terms of resolving the fight or improving their relationship.

*Helpful actions to take with siblings who are fighting* – Respectfully, give each child the time to explain what happened from her side.

Sympathise and reflect back the feelings of each child – 'It must be hard to share your brand new toy'; 'It must be hard to see your sister with a new toy that you really want to have yourself.'

If the children look like they might hurt each other, separate them. 'Oh dear, looks like we need a bit of space. Why don't you go play with your Lego in the front room and you go see what Daddy's doing in the kitchen?'

TIPS TO ENCOURAGE SHARING

1   Give the children control over how they want to share by putting them in charge of sharing something new.
2   Promote some situations in which sharing benefits everyone, e.g. putting the toy plane into the Lego structure and playing at aeroplanes together as a team.
3   Ask your more reluctant child to let the other know when she is ready to share.
4   Recognise and celebrate sharing when it happens without prompting.

## Frequently asked questions – sibling conflict

**Do children fight in the same way with their brothers and sisters as they do with their friends?**

Conflict between siblings is quite different from conflict outside of the family. Children argue more self-centredly and with more passion and hostility with their brothers and sisters than they do in other situations. Also, arguments with siblings are more likely to come to a stand-off with no resolution. When a resolution does occur, it most often involves one party submitting to the desires of the other, rather than compromise.

**Do children get better at resolving arguments with age?**

While the reasoning abilities of children develop with age, these are used to better argue one's case rather than to see the perspective of a sibling. The willingness to compromise also does not increase with age. However, research suggests that the nature of the sibling relationship goes through a profound change over adolescence, with most relationships becoming less intense as each child develops her own interests and personality outside of the home.

## Are children with siblings more advanced socially?

In one study of more than 20,000 participants, children with one or two siblings were rated by teachers as possessing better social and interpersonal skills than children with no siblings (McGuire, McHale, & Updegraff, 1996). However, there is no consistent evidence showing children with siblings demonstrate more developed social understanding or higher levels of conflict resolution or compromise.

## Does having an older sibling ease the transition to primary school?

Research has shown that having an older sibling can provide protection against the stress of life events, such as changing school, bereavement, moving house, etc. (Sandler, 1980).

## Should brothers and sisters always be treated equally?

When needs are the same, fairness would dictate that siblings should be treated equally. Of course, needs are rarely the same and all of your children are unique individuals with their own particular characters. Setting up an environment where constant direct comparisons are allowed is not going to be helpful for the overall harmony of the family. Instead, when giving out food, ask, 'How hungry are you? Would you like a lot or a little?' This can help to avoid having to count out quantities.

## Do brothers and sisters resemble each other? My two children couldn't be more different and I've heard the same from my friends.

Interestingly, research shows that parents tend to exaggerate the differences between their children. Some suggest this is related to the promotion of individual differences in an attempt to mitigate sibling rivalry. Others suggest that children are compared amongst the other members of the family, and thus any differences that are present are magnified. While parents tend to rate siblings very differently on factors such as shyness and activity level, objective reports, such as activity monitors and strangers' ratings scales, find reasonable levels of similarity between them (Saudino et al., 2004).

**Is it normal that my eldest has told me he wishes his younger brother dead?**

While this is very upsetting for a parent to hear, it is normal for siblings to feel intense anger and upset towards a brother or sister. As a parent, we can acknowledge these feelings – 'It sounds like you're really upset with him, can you tell me why (or what happened)?' – and then when things have calmed down, you can talk a little bit about some of the good times shared as a family.

**What's the best line to take when one child tells on another?**

This is a difficult one as often it's helpful to be informed of dangerous and serious rule breaking behaviour. However, it's tricky to promote family harmony when every small misdemeanour is being reported. As a parent, it is for you to judge what things should be ignored, and what things should be taken more seriously. If you routinely ignore the more minor incidents, it is likely that your children will stop coming to you with them.

## Resources

Buhrmester, D., & Furman, W. (1990). Perceptions of sibling relationships during middle childhood and adolescence. *Child Development*, *61*(5), 1387–1398.

McGuire, S., McHale, S. M., & Updegraff, K. (1996). Children's perceptions of the sibling relationship in middle childhood: Connections within and between family relationships. *Personal Relationships*, *3*(3), 229–239. http://doi.org/10.1111/j.1475-6811.1996.tb00114.x

Sandler, I. N. (1980). Social support resources, stress, and maladjustment of poor children. *American Journal of Community Psychology*, *8*(1), 41–52. http://doi.org/10.1007/BF00892280

Saudino, K., Wertz, A., Gagne, J., & Chawla, S. (2004). Night and day: Are siblings as different in temperament as parents say they are? *Journal of Personality and Social Psychology*, *87*(5), 698–706. http://doi.org/10.1097/OPX.0b013e3182540562

Stocker, C., Dunn, J., & Plomin, R. (1989). Sibling relationships: Links with child temperament, maternal behavior, and family structure. *Child Development*, *60*(3), 715–727. http://doi.org/10.2307/1130737

# Index

academic success 145
ADHD (attention deficit hyperactivity disorder) 129–139; causes of 136–137; clumsy social skills 134; defiant behaviour 134; diagnosis 130; features across all children with 133–134; frequently asked questions 137–138; friendships in children with 134; girls with 135–136, 138; hyperactive and impulsive 132–133; inattentive type 130–131; and low self-esteem 133, 135, 137; coping behaviours 135; incentive motivation 134; prescribing of Ritalin 136–137; supporting children with 137; tests for 138; working memory 134
alarms, moisture sensitive 26
American Academy of Pediatrics (AAP) 45, 46
attachment 96; behaviour 96–97; parenting 100; supporting 100; theory 96, 101
attention: development of focused 131; lavishing young children with 9; TV watching and influence on 54

baby: arrival of a new 160; babbling 75, 79; led feeding 39–40; monitors 21; signing 79
Bandura, Albert 8
bed sharing 23–24, 28
bed wetting 25–26, 137
bilingual children 107–115; bilingual advantage 107–108; defining bilingualism 108–109; frequently

asked questions 112–114; language development 110; learning through television or radio 53; one person, one language approach 109–110; raising children to be 109–110, 110–112
birth spacing 157–158
BMI and links with screen time 47
books, sharing with preschoolers 65–66
bottle feeding *see* breastfeeding vs. formula feeding
Bowlby, John 96
boys' underperformance at school 147–148
brain development and screen time 49
breast milk: and boost to immune system 40; composition 35, 39, 40; mother's diet and impact on 39; and protection from ear infections 40; recommendations for 34–35
breastfeeding vs. formula feeding 33–43; baby-led feeding 39–40; and baby weight gain 41; bonding 41; breast milk composition 35, 39, 40; difficulties with breastfeeding 33, 37–38; frequently asked questions 39–42; giving both formula and breast milk 41; hormones and milk secretion 41–42; infant formula composition 35; IQ levels and 36, 37; making choices 34; problems with research 36–37; reasons mothers stop breastfeeding 38; recommendations 34–35; returning to work and breastfeeding 38–39;